W9-APM-466

MAY 20 '91	DATE DUE	
APR 7 '93		
APR 30 1993		
OCT 17 1995		
NOV 07 1995		

Managing
Smart

Managing Smart

A No-Gimmick Handbook of Management Techniques That Work

ARTHUR P. BRIEF

GERALD TOMLINSON

Lexington Books

D.C. Heath and Company • Lexington, Massachusetts • Toronto

Library of Congress Cataloging-in-Publication Data

Brief, Arthur P., 1946–
Managing smart.

Bibliography: p.
Includes index.
1. Management.   2. Organizational behavior.
3. Personnel management.   I. Tomlinson, Gerald,
1933–   II. Title.
HD31.B7396   1987   658.3   85-45978
ISBN-0-669-12654-3 (alk. paper)

Published simultaneously in Canada
Printed in the United States of America
Casebound International Standard Book Number: 0-669-12654-3
Library of Congress Catalog Card Number: 85-45978

The paper used in this publication meets
the minimum requirements of American National Standard
for Information Sciences—Permanence of Paper
for Printed Library Materials, ANSI Z39.48-1984.

ISBN 0-669-12654-3

87 88 89 90   8 7 6 5 4 3 2

*To those who have produced
the knowledge that made it possible
for this book to be written.*

Contents

Preface

AMERICAN business needs smart management as never before. Most individual managers are smart. If they weren't, they wouldn't be managers. But it's one thing to be smart and quite another to manage smart.

As a rule, when intelligent, forward-looking managers are supplied with the knowledge and techniques to manage smart, they can and do. The intent of this book is to supply you with that knowledge and those techniques.

Managing Smart is solidly based on studies of organizational behavior. As with much research in all fields, valuable studies of management tend to fall through the cracks, while what is popularly written about management is all too often trendy and untried. This book explains the management practices that have repeatedly been shown to *work*.

A revolution in how Americans manage is not called for. On the contrary, many of the lessons in this book are drawn from the study of successful American management practices. What is needed is some way to ensure that these practices are more widely used. *Managing Smart* is dedicated to that goal.

1

Back to Basics

The Four Key Factors

Four key elements govern managerial success:

1. Luck
2. Ease
3. Effort
4. Ability

It's popular to regard managers as calculating people who choose rationally from among alternative courses of action, cannily picking the best possible option, the shrewd move, the one with the highest probability of success. Well, that description is sometimes accurate, but not always. In many cases, the odds simply aren't known. As a manager, you fervently wish to choose the option that gives you the best shot at winning, but you just don't know what it is. You have to base your choice on a hunch, on intuition, on the toss of a coin.

Managers frequently operate in an environment of uncertainty. You can't change that. It goes with the territory, furnishing both challenges and opportunities. It's fine to say that over the years, all else being equal, everything will balance out. But the real-world truth is this: All else is *never* equal in the hurly-burly of business management. Like it or not, *luck* plays a role.

So does the *ease* of your managerial task. Some management jobs are easier than others. If you run a business that markets a high-quality, low-cost product with high demand and few competitors (how did you get into *that* terrific position?), your job is a cinch. On the other hand, what if you are running a business that markets a product exactly like everybody else's? Your task is a lot tougher. You may still succeed brilliantly, but your success will be much harder won than it would be if you were under no competitive pressure.

In general, you have little to say about the level of difficulty of your job. Therefore, ease, like luck, is pretty much beyond your control. This raises an interesting paradox. Managers often blame their failures on bad luck or lack of resources. Not surprisingly, they point to these uncontrollable factors—to their unlucky stars—and not to themselves for their lack of success. No one wants to hand down his or her own indictment. Yet rarely do these same managers credit luck or point to the ease of their assignment when they succeed. Now, clearly, it should work both ways. Good as well as bad luck must play a part. Easy as well as demanding tasks must have an effect. And of course they do. These two uncontrollable factors, luck and ease, are legitimate components of success.

Two other factors enter into the equation. Both can be controlled. The first is *effort*. A common assumption is that competitive businesses require managers with more ambition than that implied by a nine-to-five routine. Good managers have to put in time and plenty of it. Up to a point, this makes sense. Effort does influence managerial success. A lazy manager finds favor with no one. But the case for effort can be, and frequently is, overstated. Some managers are even evaluated according to the amount of time and sweat they put in, rather than according to their actual accomplishments. That shouldn't happen in a well-run organization. Managerial effort, and the underlying motivation to do well that it implies, are prerequisites to success, not success itself.

The fourth factor, *ability*, includes both natural talent and acquired skills. Ability is visible. It can be assessed. Ability shows clearly in how you go about doing your job.

What kind of people do you select to work for you?

What do you want these people to accomplish?

When do you want them to accomplish it?

And most central . . .

Why do you want them to accomplish it?

Ability is a priceless and controllable asset, and it is the very essence of managing smart. You can choose (or not choose) to develop your ability. You can choose (or not choose) to apply it. Given its significance in management success, ability in all its aspects requires close attention. How do you identify it? How do you nurture it? How do you use it? How do you assess it? This book concentrates on developing and applying managerial ability.

Introducing the Smart Manager

Like every able and intelligent manager, you have inherited some of your ability from your forebears. Without getting into the nature versus nurture controversy, it's safe to say that genes have their effects. But they don't mean everything, or anywhere near it. Native ability, or inborn talent, is emphatically not enough. There are legions of failed geniuses. You have to work with your ability, shape it, develop it.

Through experience and study, you can make great strides as a manager. Experience is usually touted as the supreme teacher. Baseball's Earl Weaver, the Baltimore Orioles' manager for many years, put it amusingly in the title of his autobiography: *It's What You Learn After You Know It All That Counts.* But experience can be supplemented by study, and it should be. The question is, given the twenty-four-hour limit of our days, what should a manager study?

Three Ps of Knowledge

On-the-job ability requires knowledge, however it is acquired. There are three basic kinds of knowledge you need to master:

- Product
- Process
- People

Product. A product can be tangible object, like a motorcycle or a microchip, or it can be a service. Most managers don't need to possess the most complete product knowledge of anybody in their business units. However, they do need to have a deep, accurate understanding of the essential characteristics of their product. Additionally, they need to know how those characteristics position the product in the marketplace. Sound marketing decisions depend on such knowledge—and sound marketing decisions are what produce revenue.

Process. Revenue coming in is only half the story. There is also money going out, money being spent to produce the product or provide the service. Expenditures, and thus profits, are directly influenced by a manager's knowledge of process—the mechanics of transforming some kind of input into a marketable good or service. Again, you, the manager, don't have to be the supreme expert on every intricacy that leads to the final result, but you do have to know enough about all aspects of the process to make sound decisions.

One clear advantage gained by the effective management of process is this: It gives you the opportunity to minimize costs. And that isn't the only competitive advantage. Decisions about production processes affect essential product characteristics. They influence the product's market position. The right process decisions lead, at least in part, to the right product characteristics, which lead in turn to the right market position and, ideally, to ultimate sales success. If that sounds a bit ponderous, look at it this way: Product and process are intimately tied. You need to know something, but not necessarily everything, about both.

People. The third kind of knowledge needed is like the third side of a triangle. It's essential. Without it, you have no triangle at all.

Until the Age of Robotics is fully upon us and managers can control events with a keyboard, a knowledge of people will be a vital resource in the smart manager's arsenal. Indeed, the application of a thorough knowledge of people precedes the making of product and process decisions. More than that, it largely shapes the outcomes of those decisions. As a manager, you depend on others. You have to. It's your job description. It's what management is all about.

Focusing on People

Your work as a manager requires you to select, train, motivate, and retain the people you want in the positions you want them in. Your personnel department can and should help out, but these tasks are too central to be wholly delegated. A good manager is preeminently a leader. A leader by definition must have followers, and not just any old followers will do. You want dedicated, enthusiastic followers, people who see purpose and value in your mutual venture and take pride in it.

At this point, you may be wondering why some of the nuts-and-bolts topics seem to have been neglected here. You may have noticed that accounting and finance are not mentioned. Why? Accounting and finance are important, to be sure. They give you an objective means of evaluating the interaction of product, process, and people. They provide information.

Now, the information you have as a manager has a great deal to do with your decisions, the results of which will be reflected in the bottom line. Accounting and finance provide the analytic tools for making many of those decisions. Consequently, it isn't surprising that accounting and finance assignments are often found along the road to senior management positions.

Yet analytic ability alone is seldom enough to produce managerial success. Just as the world's best chisel won't make an average stonecarver into Michelangelo, neither will the tools of accounting and finance make a mediocre manager into Lee Iacocca. Whatever your level of management, you must understand how to *use* the tools of accounting and finance, how to react to the numbers they generate.

It all comes down to your knowledge of people. This doesn't mean that you need a degree in psychology or that you should rush out to join an Est group. But is does mean that, to the extent possible, and in a way that you find rewarding, you should sharpen your knowledge of people.

The Three Basic Rs

Millions of words have been written on the subject of managing people. What can be said that will be startlingly original? Not a lot. Breezy management authors and pricey consultants to the contrary, there are few if any dazzling managerial secrets, few if any one-shot fixes. What there is, however—and in part because of the flood of magic-formula solutions—is a real need for returning to, and reviewing, the basics.

In other words, we need to look at what actually *works*. That's the starting point. William J. Bennett, President Reagan's secretary of education, recently addressed the question as it applies to teaching and learning. His department published "a distillation of a large body of scholarly research" in an attempt to show, in the no-nonsense title of the report—*What Works*. Bennett's aim was not to bound off down yet another unmapped trail to greatness, excellence, quality, or leadership—noble, ringing words, but slippery abstractions that tend to remain so—but rather to synthesize what we already know about teaching and learning. Practical and unglamorous, it's the nitty-gritty stuff that classroom experience, not airy speculation, has validated. In essence, naturally, it's the "three Rs."

There are three Rs in management too, and they're just as basic to managing people as readin', 'ritin', and 'rithmetic are to educating children. The three Rs of managing people are:

- Require
- Review
- Reward

As the words suggest, these basics are concerned with:

Figuring out what you should expect from your employees, and communicating those expectations to them

Determining whether your employees have met your expectations, and then communicating that message to them

Allocating scarce resources such as raises and promotions to employees who have best met your expectations

You, the smart manager, can control employee performance. By applying the three basic Rs, you can help your employees make the right choices about:

Where they should apply their efforts

How much effort they should put into the tasks at hand

How long they should persist in applying the effort

The goal is a motivated work force whose energies are appropriately directed. It's an easy goal to state, but you are sure to encounter some fire-breathing dragons along the way. Stephen Crane, the great American writer, caught the essence of the problem in his poem "The Wayfarer."

> *The wayfarer,*
> *Perceiving the pathway to truth,*
> *Was struck with astonishment.*
> *It was thickly grown with weeds.*
> *"Ha," he said,*
> *"I see that no one has passed here*
> *In a long time."*
> *Later he saw that each weed*
> *Was a singular knife.*
> *"Well," he mumbled at last,*
> *"Doubtless there are other roads."*

Take your pick—dragons or weeds or maybe nothing more hazardous than office politics. Whatever the obstacle is, you are sure to encounter it. And you may come to wonder about the truth of the three Rs. You may begin to suspect that the three Rs work better on paper than in practice.

Why They're Basic

Since at least the turn of the century, the three Rs have been regarded as the bedrock of sound management practice. Important figures in business history such as Frederick W. Taylor, Chester Barnard, and Alfred P. Sloan preached their virtues decades ago. The world has changed since then, but truth has not. To require, to review, and to reward are as useful to managers now as they ever were. The three Rs are not snake oil offered from the back of a gaudy high-tech wagon by the latest traveling management expert. They are basic lessons learned in the evolution of the modern corporation, the time-proven management techniques that produce results.

And they are basic in another sense. They are easy to learn. They provide you with the big picture, a general outline that can be filled in with details that you acquire throughout your entire management career.

A sophisticated body of behavioral-science literature exists concerning each and all of the three Rs. In this book, you will find the main ideas of the most relevant literature presented in concise form. The intent here is to give you, quickly and readably, the essence of what you need to know to apply the three Rs effectively.

A Fourth R: Respect

The three Rs are fundamental. Properly applied, they will reliably lead your employees to meet expectations. They will make your work force dependable. But dependable performance, important as it is, is not always enough. You also want your employees to act spontaneously and innovatively so as to capitalize on chance, on the fortuitous turn of events in an uncertain business environment. Such performance cannot be programmed. It can be achieved only by applying the fourth R: *Respect*.

Respect implies trust. "An organization without trust," wrote Warren Bennis and Burt Nanus in *Leaders: The Strategies for Taking Charge*, "is more than an anomaly, it's a misnomer, a dim creature of Kafka's imagination. Trust implies accountability, predictability, reliability."

Respect and trust involve positioning—making your own position clear and consistent, and letting employees know exactly what is expected of them. As a manager, you must position yourself so that you can hold your employees in high regard. You must also position your employees so that they can contribute optimally to your business unit's effectiveness.

This isn't always easy. The organizational chart may be redrawn, circumstances may change, people may move. You may find yourself in a position where you cannot honestly say that you respect your employees. In that situation, some repositioning is called for. As used here, the word *repositioning* is a synonym for hiring, transferring, and firing. If you inherited a swamp, you'll have to clear it, alligators (or dragons) and all. The task isn't pleasant, but it's essential. Then, given the opportunity, you'll want to hire employees you *do* respect. Once you are on the right course with the right people, you'll want to develop their talent to its fullest potential.

Self-management for Success

Your work as a manager involves directing people. One of those people is yourself. On the job, your personal success and that of the business unit you manage are closely tied. But you can do far more to facilitate your own growth and development than just to apply the four Rs to your subordinates.

One thing you can do is apply the four Rs to yourself. Since the 1960s, clinical psychologists have trained their clients to use the four Rs as a therapeutic strategy to help them cope with such problems as excess eating, smoking, and drinking. As a self-management technique, this application of the four Rs is well worth considering, and it will be looked at later.

Managing smart also includes acquiring and using power while maintaining a climate of trust. Weak managers don't succeed. But neither do strong ones who use their power in a heavy-handed or overbearing way that fosters an atmosphere of fear and insecurity. You must strike a delicate balance if you are to avoid being viewed as either a wimp or a brute.

A lot has been written about career management. Most of it is too shallow to be of use to anyone except a recent high school graduate. What remains tends to be draconian. Typically, it advises career-minded people to sacrifice much of their present life for some distant, vaguely defined form of success. There are, nonetheless, a few practical principles to be gleaned from the generally depleted field of career-management research.

The end of this book gets into the crucial issue of impression management—how to be your own best cheerleader. Mastering and applying the four Rs will contribute to your success as a manager, but you have to do a certain amount of self-promotion, too. That may seem unfair, but it's a fact of business life. With everyone else cheering (for himself or herself), you should not keep your own achievements a secret. To manage smart, you have to build an image. Chapters 13 and 14 explain how.

And Away We Go!

This chapter has been an overview, defining the boundaries of the territory to be covered, pointing out many of the landmarks you will see along the way. Some of the terrain may be familiar. Don't be put off if it is, for that's a good sign. What it suggests is that the path you're now following is the right one.

On the other hand, much of the material about the fourth R, respect, will probably be new to you. That's also good. Venture into the unknown. "Courage," said Amelia Earhart, "is the price that life exacts for granting peace." Dan Rather may have had something like that in mind as he gazed into the eye of the corporate storm at CBS in 1986, ending his nightly newscast for a time with the single word, "Courage."

Ten Points to Remember

1. There is no single magic ingredient for managerial success, but rather a number of interactive elements.

2. Four key factors affect managerial success: (1) luck, (2) ease, (3) effort, and (4) ability.

3. Luck and ease are uncontrollable factors, but effort and ability are within your power to develop and improve.

4. Ability, which includes both talent and acquired skills, is the main factor in the success equation.

5. As a smart manager, you need a thorough knowledge of the three Ps of your business unit: Product, Process, and People.

6. A knowledge of people is vitally important in making decisions regarding product and process.

7. Accounting and finance provide the analytic tools for decision making, but you must know how to use them.

8. The three Rs of managing people—Require, Review, and Reward—are fundamental to your success as a manager.

9. There is a fourth R, Respect, based on making your own position clear and consistent, and letting employees know what you expect of them.

10. Managerial effectiveness can be greatly enhanced by good self-management, including image building.

2

Dynamics of Performance

Y OUNG employees can be hard to manage, as many older managers know. The youngsters complain. They make demands.
It isn't necessarily true that the young employees have a different set
of work values from their older associates. They often work hard
enough. Usually they are unhappy because their expectations are not
being met. They blame management for their lack of rapid progress.

But it isn't management's fault. Young people, because of their
lack of work experience, are often naive. They expect too much responsibility too quickly. Recently minted MBAs, for instance, typically expect their first employers to put them in positions of consid-
erable authority and sensitivity. Few managers are so foolish as to
oblige. The risk is too great. The young MBA may be a genuine
world-beater, but the manager doesn't know that yet, not until sus-
tained performance proves it.

As people mature, their expectations become more realistic. They
have seen the business environment up close. They have had the
opportunity to prove themselves. Managers can assign them with
greater confidence to more demanding positions. For all these reasons, management often meets the expectations of older employees
better than those of younger ones. Consequently, older employees
tend to be more satisfied and easier to manage.

Implicit in what has been said is that all employees have a set of
expectations. They look to management to fulfill those expectations.

The Unwritten Contract

How do you, as a manager, fulfill employees' expectations? What do
you offer? Chester Barnard, an executive with AT&T during the

1930s, said that you provide the employee with what he called inducements. In return for these inducements, employees make contributions to the business unit. Inducements plus contributions create an unwritten contract between management and employees.

This contract, even though not spelled out on an individual basis, is quite specific as to what inducements are offered to the employee. Company policies are usually codified. Some of the inducements, such as pay and fringe benefits, are explicit and generally written out. The employee has an accurate picture of inducements.

Not so (or at least not always so) with contributions. That side of the contract is often more vague. You've told your employees the obvious requirements of the job, of course. They know the working hours. They know whether or not overtime will be expected. But are they fully aware of the particular kinds of contributions they must make to fulfill their obligations? It isn't safe to assume that they know unless they have been told, straightforwardly, unmistakably.

A Fair Day's Pay . . .

Everybody agrees with the saying, "A fair day's pay for a fair day's work." Right? Wrong. The problem is not so much with the statement itself—in principle, nobody opposes motherhood or apple pie either—but with the interpretation of it. While the inducements are pretty clear, the expected contributions may not be. What is a fair day's work?

Obviously, it depends on the job. Jobs vary a great deal, and it's easier to quantify the results of some jobs than it is of others. Regardless of the type of job, though, most employees have a general understanding of what tasks they're supposed to perform. But how definite is that understanding? Do the employees know just how much they have to do, and when? In many cases, the answer is decidedly *no*.

The Gansevoort Company (not its real name) is a retailing firm in New York City. The company has a training program in which newly hired sales personnel learn the tasks they will be required to perform. The explanation they're given is complete and understandable. Gansevoort training goes one step farther. It informs these employees that to keep their jobs they will have to produce "an acceptable level of sales volume."

Now, here's the catch: They don't tell their employees exactly what constitutes "an acceptable level of sales volume." The quota is either ambiguous or subjective. In either case, the employees have been left dangling. And this is by no means an isolated instance. A similar lack of explicit performance standards can be found in some commercial banks, insurance companies, consumer product manufacturers, and so on.

But How Much *Work?*

Daniel Katz, a noted organizational psychologist at the University of Michigan, has made some relevant observations on this issue. He defines an employee's obligations as twofold: carrying out assigned tasks *and* meeting certain levels of performance. Merely doing the job isn't enough. As a manager, you must be able to depend on your employees to do their jobs *and do them well*.

As Katz points out, management must specify the performance levels it will accept. If you neglect to specify those levels, you can hardly hold the employee responsible for inadequate performance. How can a Gansevoort manager credibly tell a new salesperson that she has sold too few women's dresses? On what basis? People can't be expected to meet obligations of which they are unaware.

Another example: Ted Felsen, a technical writer for a pharmaceutical company, is good but slow. Too good (in one sense) and too slow. He labors long and hard over his text, and by the time it's finished, it's brilliant—easily the best of its kind in the department. It's overdue, however. The deadline has been missed. As it happens, lateness isn't fatal in this specific project, and Ted's manager overlooks it. In fact, he says, "Great job, Ted."

No! It's *not* a great job. Ted has two parameters, quality and time. He stayed within one and strayed from the other. Under the unwritten contract, he failed to fulfill his obligations and, having done so, has now been told in effect that it's okay to fail. But it isn't. Next time, when the deadline is critical and Ted misses it, the manager will be hard put to say, "Your report is nicely written, Ted, but at this point we may as well wrap fish in it."

The Role of Strategy

"I tell my employees what performance levels I expect from them," the avuncular manager says with a touch of pride. That sounds fine, but it's probably too vague a prescription to be helpful. Performance levels need definition. They need to be carefully spelled out. This can be both a chore and a challenge. Where do these standards come from? The definition of expected performance levels stems, in most cases, from the strategy of the business unit.

The most important strategic choices a manager makes concern what goods or services the business unit will produce and in what market those products will be sold. Those strategic choices determine just about everything else that must be done to try to ensure success in the marketplace.

By the very nature of strategic decisions, you don't have to make them very often. If your business unit has had to reformulate its strategy every few months, or even every few years, the implication is strong that prior decisions were bad ones. Minor adjustments will be made periodically, of course, but frequent changes in the principal thrust of the business are a recipe for trouble and a sure sign of danger. Once the energies of your unit are mobilized and directed, you can't change course without losing a lot of distance in the competitive race.

For many managers, the role of strategist is a glamorous one. That may explain why it is sometimes overplayed. Be careful that *you* don't overplay the part. Once those infrequent decisions have been made, get on with the job of implementing them. As Terrence Daniels of W.R. Grace has said, strategic management is "20 percent conceptualization and 80 percent implementation."

Let other managers in competing businesses emphasize thinking at the expense of doing, if they want to be so foolish. That way, you can be off and running while their heads are still in the strategic clouds.

When it's time to execute strategic plans, you must specify what you want your employees to do and how well you want them to do it. That *how well* isn't a tongue-in-cheek phrase. You want them to do it perfectly, but it isn't that simple. Even as the product is launched, the answer to your how-well question may be uncertain in a competitive market. Time will provide the answer, though. The market will let you know.

Let the Market Speak

Once you identify the market in which your product will compete, your goal is to seek and maintain an advantage over your opponents.

That's easy to say, but sometimes not so easy to do. Here are four essential steps.

1. Identify your customer population. Who buys (or will buy) your goods or services? Beyond that, who uses (or will use) them?
2. Sample your customer population. Ask them to identify for you the product features by which they compare you with your competitors. Don't approach customers with a preconceived list. Let them generate the list for you.
3. For each product feature identified by your customers, determine the quality or level of performance of your competitors. Know what you're up against.
4. Set performance requirements that allow you to meet, and in some respects beat, your competition. Then let the market speak.

Let's say, for example, you run a fast-food chain, Mrs. Goodburgers. Your restaurants are apparently doing something wrong, because three or four other fast-food chains are clobbering you. You do the necessary (but belated) market research. You do a thorough competitive analysis. You conclude that your customers, although approving of your high-quality beef, want to purchase freshly cooked burgers. Since Mrs. G's burgers are sometimes cooked twenty minutes or more in advance of purchase, you decide that has to change. Wendy McBurger is usually delivering burgers within five minutes of purchase. You instruct your head of operations to reduce the time between cooking and purchase so as to match the best time of your competitors. This may mean slightly slower fast-food service at Mrs. Goodburgers, but it's clearly what your customers want. That's letting the market speak.

Rewinding the Stopwatch

Your product is what you sell, but product is only one of the three Ps. Process is important too. If the product seems to be just dandy but the bottom line isn't, look to your knowledge of process.

About seventy-five years ago, Frederick W. Taylor, a mechanical engineer and inventor, suggested finding out what constituted a fair day's work. His method was to analyze precisely what a typical worker could be expected to produce in a given amount of time, assuming that the worker was properly trained, motivated, and equipped. Taylor's analytic technique, time-and-motion study, employed a stopwatch. He was the first efficiency expert and a strong advocate of scientific management.

Taylor is also considered to be the founder of industrial engineering. For decades, his influence on American management practices was enormous; the word *Taylorism* even appears in some dictionaries. His influence waned in time, however, and the stopwatch as a management tool was laid aside. Today most industrial engineers or efficiency experts prefer to call themselves *systems engineers*. Nevertheless, they still use science and math to discover procedures for accomplishing tasks efficiently.

Except in manufacturing, today's managers have a tendency to ignore engineering techniques in establishing performance requirements. Certainly, what Thomas J. Peters and Robert H. Waterman, Jr., call the old rationalism (of Frederick W. Taylor and others) in their best-selling book, *In Pursuit of Excellence*, had plenty of negative aspects. The factory slowdown, for instance, was a direct result of standards imposed by time-and-motion studies. Yet engineering techniques can surely be used in some situations to help establish performance requirements. They should seldom be rejected out of hand unless you, the manager, have direct access to the necessary process knowledge. Taylorism is passé, but the underlying idea is perfectly sensible.

What's the Process?

Sometimes managers do have a direct knowledge of process. Here's an example: The management of a paper products company discovered that the trucks transporting its logs were being loaded well below the legal limit. As reported by Gary Latham, a consultant who specializes in helping businesses establish performance requirements, the unionized truck drivers were told to have their trucks loaded henceforth to 94 percent of the legal limit. They did, and the average net weight of loads jumped immediately from 60 percent of the legal limit to the newly required 94 percent. In nine months, that change of process saved the company more than $250,000.

In this case, the law provided the necessary process knowledge to set performance requirements. There are many ways for you to find the information needed. For example:

Manufacturers' specifications for the equipment used in production processes

Company records of past production levels

Day-to-day experience with the production process being managed

This list barely scratches the surface. Dozens of approaches are possible, whether you're processing patients, paper, or paintbrushes. You're limited only by your own efforts and imagination when it comes to identifying sources of process information that can be used as a basis for setting performance requirements.

You may think that a very good source of input is being overlooked—the employees who do the jobs for which performance standards are being set. This chapter notwithstanding, they aren't being ignored. Participatory methods of establishing performance requirements will be covered in detail when the fourth R, respect, is discussed later in the book. For now, it's imperative to emphasize *your* responsibility, management's responsibility, for setting performance requirements.

Ten Points to Remember

1. The expectations of younger employees are sometimes unrealistically high, creating problems for managers.

2. All employees have a set of expectations about their work; maturity tends to bring expectations into line with reality.

3. Managers offer inducements, while employees are expected to make contributions; an unwritten contract exists between them.

4. All employees should be made explicitly aware of the contributions they are expected to make.

5. An employee has an obligation to carry out assigned tasks and to meet minimal levels of performance.

6. You, as a manager, must clearly specify the performance levels you will accept—and then refuse to accept lower levels.

7. Business-unit strategy determines the specific kinds of performance requirements you need to put into effect.

8. Find out as accurately and completely as possible what it is that your customers want; let the market speak.

9. If industrial engineering techniques are appropriate for establishing performance standards, use them.

10. Explore various approaches for discovering process information; use the information you find as a basis for setting performance requirements.

3

Setting Performance Requirements

As the manager of a business unit, you are the sole person accountable for setting performance requirements. Setting those standards is essential to ensuring that the unit's strategy is successfully executed. You cannot delegate responsibility for making sure that these requirements are set.

This doesn't mean you have to be actively involved in setting the hundreds or even thousands of performance requirements needed. You simply don't have the time. Fortunately, there's an easy solution.

The number of levels in the management hierarchy depends on the size of your company and on its management philosophy. There are some levels, surely, which means that there are managers who report to the chief executive, other managers who report to those managers, and so on down the chain of command. When you, the business-unit manager, set performance requirements for the people reporting directly to you, the first requirement should read: "Set performance requirements for your direct reports consistent with those set for you." If that practice is adhered to all the way down the hierarchy, as it should be, you are likely to get the necessary performance requirements set.

No more than "likely"? That's right. The possibility becomes a reality only if you follow the dictates of the second and third Rs, review and reward. You must assess how well your immediate subordinates have set appropriate performance requirements for their subordinates, and so on down the line. All managers involved in the process should be rewarded, or not rewarded, in accordance with these assessments.

The main point is this: The setting of performance requirements is of necessity a top-down process. No matter how the corporate hierarchy functions in other areas, in this particular area it must operate like the U.S. Marines.

Identify the Essentials

Anyone who has tried to write performance requirements knows how tough it is. You may be perfectly aware of what you do and what your employees do, and what all of you are expected to do. But putting that information on paper can be quite a challenge.

The basic rule for setting performance requirements is to avoid the trivial. Stick to main activities. Jobs are composed of tasks. For most jobs, you could easily identify dozens of different tasks. For some, you could probably list hundreds, or thousands. A U.S. Air Force study, for instance, found that a staff nurse performs more than ten thousand different tasks. Should a hospital administrator therefore set ten thousand performance requirements for the job? Of course not. Every job has a focus. Consequently, most tasks fall into a few natural clusters of activities. Satisfactory performance within these clusters is what warrants the attention of management.

Let's look again at the job of staff nurse with its ten thousand tasks. In two different hospitals, one of the authors of this book observed that the ten thousand tasks fell quite readily into ten clusters. A ten-point set of performance requirements could satisfactorily encompass all those tasks. And ten, unlike ten thousand, is a manageable number.

What Do You Expect?

Performance requirements deal with essential clusters of activities. Very well. But the question remains, how do you identify those essential clusters?

Industrial psychology offers several proven techniques. Simpler approaches, however, are often acceptable. For a given job, you can ask yourself, "What contributions to the business unit should the employees in this job make?" Or even more straightforward: "What do I expect these employees to do?" In a way, you might view this as a top-down approach to identifying clusters. Instead of starting with the nurse's ten thousand tasks, you are starting with a few desirable major outcomes.

Notice that so far the questions about performance concern neither its quality nor its quantity. Those issues will be dealt with later. For now, you just need to identify the broad, important performance dimensions of the job.

Since some managers and some employees are likely to regard the setting of performance requirements as a burden, you should be prepared to answer objections. Some may feel that it's a needless undertaking. ("We know what we've got to do, chief.") Well, they're wrong. They know what they're doing right now on a day-to-day basis, but the scope of the job is defined in terms of the overall business strategy.

Some may feel that it's so simple as to be insulting. ("Gee, I think I sell computer software.") They're wrong, too. When taken seriously (as it should be), the identification of key performance dimensions will prove to be a very demanding assignment. Think of New York Mets' pitcher Ron Darling trying to put into a ten-point list all the physiological nuances of throwing a slider. Listing performance requirements isn't quite that hard, but it's harder than many people suppose.

It's Got to Be Observable

Diane Weiner manages a large retail outlet. One day, with a vice president at her side, she observed (without being observed) a salesclerk approach a customer. The clerk smiled pleasantly and said, "May I help you?" That was followed by polite and evidently constructive attention to the customer's wishes. Turning to the vice president, Diane said, "Now, that clerk has the right attitude." Wrong.

The salesclerk's performance was acceptable, yes. But what did it reveal about the clerk's attitude? For all Diane knows, the clerk may be sending poison-pen letters to the vice president or planting bombs in the washrooms. Granted, that's unlikely, but the possibility is worth noting. Diane cannot safely infer the clerk's attitude from the clerk's behavior. All she can assess is the observed behavior.

And that's fine. Diane doesn't know what the clerk's true attitudes are, and arguably she shouldn't even care. What ought to concern her is the performance of the clerk, not the underlying attitudes on which the performance is presumably based.

Stating performance requirements in terms of attitudes or personality traits is a common mistake. No matter how important you believe these traits to be, you cannot observe them. You can observe only the behaviors they presumably produce. It follows that you have to rely on observable behaviors as indicators of performance. There's really no other way.

Each important performance dimension of a job can be defined as a kind of behavior or as an outcome of behavior. Consider the example of the salesclerk. Behaviorally, the performance requirement can be stated like this: "Services customers in a prompt and helpful manner." An outcome of this behavior could be customer satisfaction and a specified, clearly defined volume of sales.

The main reason for the behavioral approach to performance dimensions is that the results can be observed and measured. As the next chapter explains, the second R, review, demands objective measurement. You can't review your employees' performance with any plausibility or accuracy unless you know, rather than just feel, how well they have done their jobs. Levels of achievement have to be assessed. Performance requirements based on observable behaviors and outcomes make such measurement feasible.

Control Equals Accountability

The question of accountability enters into the setting of performance requirements. In recent years, accountability has become a buzzword in American education. Teachers, it is said, should be held accountable for whether their students learn or fail to learn. The legitimate concern that teachers have about this issue is one that faces you as a manager when you set performance requirements.

Once again, let's look at an example from retailing. One of the senior author's clients in the department-store business holds a position called *department manager.* Each department manager is responsible for supervising the salesclerks assigned to his or her department. This is a demanding job, but note what it does *not* include:

A *buyer* selects, purchases, and prices the merchandise sold in the department.

A *display manager* handles the placement of merchandise and the general appearance and layout of the department.

A *personnel manager* hires salesclerks for the department and determines their compensation.

In short, the only responsibility delegated to the department manager is that of direct supervision of the salesclerks. There's nothing wrong with that, and it works well in practice. However, the CEO of the firm, ignoring the narrow scope of the department manager's job, has repeatedly tried to hold department managers responsible for the bottom-line results of their departments.

You can see the difficulty. Department managers exert little direct control over profits. They don't select, price, or display the merchandise in their departments. They don't even choose and compensate their employees. If the buyer, display manager, and personnel manager are a trio of dunces (or, in the nature of these things, if just one of them deserves the cap), the department manager takes the rap.

The key phrase in the last paragraph is *direct control*. For you to demand accountability, the employee must exercise a reasonable amount of direct control. If an employee doesn't have direct control over one or more performance requirements, then the requirement should not be set. It is simply unfair to hold employees accountable for results that are beyond their control.

An example from manufacturing underscores this point. In "Sigafoos Industries," the product manager is responsible for determining the exact nature of a new product. The plant manager is responsible for producing a product to those specifications. The marketing manager must persuade the public to buy the product. These people work closely together and are generally cooperative.

Nevertheless, suppose their new product fails, as happens now and then. The human reaction of the product manager is to suggest that the quality of the manufactured item was not exactly Rolls–Roycean and that the people in marketing should perhaps take up organic gardening. The human reaction of the plant manager is to suspect miscalculation in product management and sloth in marketing. The human reaction of the marketing manager is to wonder how the guy from Edsel landed a spot in product management, while the guy who used to run GM's Lordstown plant was worming his way in as a Sigafoos plant manager.

That's overstated, but not by much. And the only objective way to sort out the truth in such matters is to have an adequate system of performance requirements tied to accountability.

If the fulfillment of a performance requirement is directly dependent on an employee's effort and ability, then accountability is justified. This doesn't mean that the employee must exercise total control. Most employees depend in part on their co-workers, the equipment they use, and even on the corporate image. Determining what is a reasonable degree of direct control is a matter of judgment. The judgment needs to be based on careful analysis of the true role of effort and ability in producing results. It should not be based on wishful thinking—on what you as a manager might like to require, but rather on what is, in fact, fair.

Make It Specific

A performance requirement must provide specific details. How many times have you told an employee, "This is an important assignment, a really big one. I want you to do your best"? If you're like most managers, you've probably said something like that so many times you can't remember.

Maybe it's a legacy of the locker room. "Win one for the Gipper!" But those Notre Dame football players had already been drilled on details within an inch of their lives, while your employees probably haven't been.

According to research by Edwin Locke and his associates, every time you set such a vague, do-your-best performance requirement, you're wasting your breath. Locke, a professor of management and psychology at the University of Maryland, has repeatedly found that employees who are assigned specific, detailed performance requirements outperform those who are given vague, back-slapping, do-your-best requirements.

You can and should spell out how much work and what level of quality you expect from your employees. The more precise the requirements, the better, because vague performance requirements simply don't motivate the effort you want from your people. Your employees will respond, however, to specific requests, and they'll respond in the way you want them to. While vague requirements create ambiguity and impede performance, detailed requirements supply the clarity that's necessary for workers to move ahead with confidence. People like to know what you expect of them. Most employees are ready to do their best on any assignment, if they know point by point what that "best" is.

Challenges, Challenges, Challenges

Some managers are afraid to ask too much from their employees. They seem to fear that if performance requirements are set too high, employees will reject them out of hand and not try at all. In fact, research has shown that the risks involved in setting requirements that are too low are greater than those involved in setting requirements that are too high.

Again, Dr. Locke's work is on target. His findings clearly indicate that the more challenging (or difficult) the requirement, the higher the level of employee performance. Ask for an ounce of effort, and you'll get it. But ask for a pound instead of an ounce, and you're likely to get that, too. At least you'll get much more than an ounce. In general, people are willing to perform better, to work harder.

In 1983 a study by the noted pollster Daniel Yankelovich found that American workers, by and large, see themselves as willing and able to work harder. They don't do it because management doesn't ask them to, or because greater effort doesn't seem to be worthwhile. These findings suggest that American managers can safely ask more from their employees. And, as Locke points out, if they ask more, they'll get more.

This prescription should carry a small warning label, however. It assumes that your workers are being underutilized. They probably are. Given the statistical fact of steadily decreasing productivity in the United States, it's a pretty safe bet that most workers in most jobs could do more than they're now doing. But it's not a sure thing. Certain workers in dynamic fields—communications and computer technology come readily to mind—may be working to their full capacity, or in some cases beyond it. This should be evident to a perceptive manager. Trying to raise performance requirements for these workers would be counterproductive.

But your first assumption should be that more effort from your employees is reasonable, desirable, and obtainable. If you believe that to be the case, don't be afraid to challenge them with difficult performance requirements. Being a softy is not managing smart.

Time-bound, Not Hidebound

"Go, sir, gallop, and don't forget that the world was made in six days. You can ask me for anything you like, except time."

Those words were spoken nearly two centuries ago by Napoleon Bonaparte. Time has always seemed too short to people of high purpose. Thomas A. Edison's efforts to cut down on the amount of time he spent sleeping are legendary. Time is as critical in business as it is in war, science, politics, or any other endeavor.

In setting performance requirements, you must be concerned with time. There are two aspects to consider.

First, some, if not most, performance requirements should be time-bound. That is to say, you should set realistic deadlines. Let's say you want an increase in sales volume, a reduction in turnover, or an improvement in return on investment. Any performance requirement for any one of these goals is meaningless unless it includes a time frame. Without a time frame, employees can all too easily respond to a negative performance evaluation by saying, "Oh, I thought you wanted those results *next* quarter." That's probably not true, but what can you say?

Second, all performance requirements need to be periodically reviewed. Market conditions change, and as they do, you should adjust whatever requirements are based on the market. Setting performance requirements should be viewed as an evolutionary process. What makes sense as a minimum requirement in the 1980s may be entirely inappropriate in the 1990s.

Never assume that a performance requirement set more than two or three years ago is correct for today. It may well be outdated. On the other hand, some managers maintain that their business environments are so turbulent and unpredictable that even short-term performance requirements cannot be set with any degree of confidence. That just isn't true unless matters are completely out of hand. In admitting such uncertainty, a manager is coming very close to admitting failure.

Don't do it. Don't cop out by blaming madness in the boardroom or the marketplace. Study your business environment carefully. Apply your best effort and ability to understanding what's happening there. No business environment is quite so tempestuous that Monday morning's truths are Tuesday afternoon's lies.

Ten Points to Remember

1. Setting performance requirements is a top-down process; you, the manager, are responsible for making sure they are set.

2. Performance requirements cannot deal with all tasks involved in a job, but instead must focus on clusters of activities.

3. In identifying performance requirements, begin by asking yourself general questions about what your employees are expected to accomplish.

4. Since not all employees like the idea of performance requirements, take time to explain their purpose and value.

5. Performance requirements must be stated in terms of observable behaviors, not attitudes or personality traits.

6. Employees can be held accountable for meeting performance requirements only in areas where they exercise a reasonable degree of direct control.

7. Be as specific and detailed as possible in stating performance requirements; vague requirements don't motivate people.

8. In general, if you make performance requirements difficult rather than easy, employee response will be positive.

9. Performance requirements should include realistic deadlines.

10. Review performance requirements for each job at least every couple of years, because circumstances change.

4

The Art of Appraisal

PEOPLE naturally want to know how well they're doing on the job. They want to know if they're meeting the performance requirements. Their concern in this matter is far from idle curiosity. Doing a satisfactory job is a prerequisite for advancement, and in many cases for even keeping their job. In addition, an employee's job performance is likely to be one of the underpinnings of his or her self-esteem. Repeated successes on the job contribute to strong, positive feelings of self-worth, while repeated failures lead to a shaky, negative self-image. Knowing that you are doing well as an employee fosters the belief that you are in control of an important part of your life. And the feeling of being in control is something nearly everyone wants.

All employees seek information about their job performance, although in some people the need for this information is stronger than in others. Certain groups of employees seem especially eager to find out how well they are doing. These groups are newly hired workers, professional and technical personnel, and—yes—managers. Even Mayor Koch of New York used to chirp, "How'm I doing?"

The reason these three particular groups want to know how they rate on the job is this: Their work role is ambiguous. They aren't entirely sure what is expected of them. They may not know for certain how to meet even the known expectations. They may not be fully aware of what will happen if they meet (or fail to meet) these expectations.

Unlike the union bricklayer, who knows exactly what performance is required and how to go about accomplishing it, new employees, professionals, managers, and others without rigid job specifications need feedback.

Performance appraisal helps to clear up the ambiguities.

Three Reasons for Appraisals

If employees need to know how well they're doing, so does management. It's next to impossible to improve (or even maintain) performance levels without having a written set of trustworthy performance appraisals. These appraisals have to be fair and accurate.
More than that, they have to be *seen* as being fair and accurate by
employees and managers alike.

There are three essential reasons to have a performance appraisal
data base:

1. *Allocating rewards.* If top raises are to go to top performers, you
   have to know who the top performers are. Gut feelings won't do.
2. *Identifying training needs.* Perhaps an employee needs to learn a
   new computer program in order to function efficiently, and he or
   she hasn't learned it; you need a formal way of finding that out.
3. *Making sound personnel moves.* When the time comes to make decisions on promotion, transfer, or placement, you need all the
   personnel information you can get; much of it should come from
   appraisals.

A fourth reason is worth mentioning, too. Trustworthy performance appraisal data can help your business fulfill its legal obligations in the area of equal employment opportunity. This is not something to be taken lightly. Fair and accurate performance appraisal
data make it easier to combat unintended bias, or the appearance of
bias, in making personnel decisions.

The Easy Way Out

Now, if such a solid case can be made for performance appraisals,
why do so many managers do such a haphazard job (and research
shows they do) in determining how well their employees are per-

forming and in letting the employees know where they stand? You probably know the answers already:

Management doesn't see the importance of collecting performance data. You've heard the familiar refrain: "We all know what we're doing here. This is a first-rate company with first-rate people. Who needs all the extra paperwork? We've got too much red tape now."

Management doesn't know how to collect the necessary data.

Management has had experience with a poorly designed appraisal system, and therefore believes that any systematic attempt to collect performance data is a waste of time.

Management wouldn't use a performance data base even if it had one, so one is never put in place.

Each of these answers is understandable on its own terms, although the last one is the kind that annoys management consultants. If you don't have the data, you can't make a judgment, after all. And not making a judgment can have seductive charms. It keeps the peace, doesn't it?

Sure, it's easier to avoid discussing poor performance with an employee than it is to sit there face-to-face and lay the problems on the line.

Sure, it's easier to allocate awards equally rather than to differentiate between high and low performers. Interestingly and inevitably, the higher the percentage of low performers you have working for you, the more support you will have for this "democratic" system.

Sure, it's easier to promote the most senior employee instead of trying to find the most qualified person. It even lends a certain stability to the business, although sometimes at great cost.

You can see that the easy way out has its appeal. But that appeal is more than offset by its drawbacks—by the dishonesty of not leveling with employees, the unfairness of not rewarding exceptional performance, the stodginess of not promoting a junior employee over a senior employee when performance clearly dictates it.

To come full circle: Performance appraisal is necessary. For one thing, employees want to know how well they are doing. For another, successful management demands that performance data be collected and used. The second R, review, assumes that you will assess your employees' performance and provide feedback to them concerning it.

Formal or Informal?

The great majority of performance appraisals are informal. These appraisals are the occasional, unstructured ones that you make now and then as you observe an employee's job performance. If you pass the results along to the employee—"Great job on the Microdaft account, Brian"—this feedback also tends to be ad hoc and fragmentary.

Formal appraisals, on the other hand, ordinarily involve set procedures, standardized forms, and scheduled interviews. They occur at regular intervals—once or twice a year, as a rule—and employees come to expect them.

Which of the two kinds should you use? That's a heads-I-win-tails-you-lose kind of question. You should use *both* kinds, for both are valuable. Informal appraisals are necessary to support a formal system, and even if they weren't, they would occur anyway as a normal part of your interaction with employees. It's hard to imagine a business in which informal assessment doesn't play a role.

Using Informal Assessment

Informal assessments support formal systems in a number of ways. One obvious way is to provide the incremental particulars on which you base your formal appraisals. Some of these particulars are based on observation. You see what's going on. You may or may not transmit your reactions immediately to the employee in the form of praise or criticism. Whether you do or not, the impressions you form of the employee will eventually be captured in the formal appraisal process.

Another role of informal appraisal is to keep employees up-to-date on how well they're doing. If formal appraisal is a yearly event, as it often is, informal appraisals will reveal that performance has sky-rocketed or nosedived long before the next formal session.

Making ad hoc assessments does more than give you and your

employee some useful information. It ensures that there will be no shocks when the formal appraisal rolls around. The surprise and disbelief that sometimes accompany a formal appraisal will be lessened if informal assessment has laid the groundwork.

A third advantage of informal appraisal is that it helps you to regulate more closely the day-to-day job performance of your employees. If their performance meets or exceeds requirements, you can commend them for their hard work, thus providing some motivation to keep it up. If their performance falls short of your expectations, you can tell them so and initiate immediately the coaching and counseling necessary to get them back on track.

Formal Systems: Accuracy and Power

As useful as an informal performance appraisal system is, it doesn't eliminate the need for a formal system. The most distinctive features of a formal system are its rigid structure and its fixed but infrequent timing. Two other less obvious features are what make the formal system a necessity, however. The first is accuracy; the second is power.

If your formal appraisal system is appropriately designed and used, it will yield more valid assessments of an employee's job performance than you can ever get through informal means. This is not to suggest that a formal system is invariably accurate and powerful. There are good formal systems and bad ones. For managerial success, you must have a carefully devised and structured system—and you must know how to use it.

If the formal system produces accurate performance appraisals, you will have gone a long way toward establishing employees' trust in it. Then, too, accuracy creates faith on the part of management. As a manager, you will feel safer relying on the data base if you are convinced of its validity.

When the formal appraisal system and its resulting assessments are used in making important personnel decisions—as they should be—the power of the system is demonstrated. No one can miss that power, or discount it, when the allocation of pay increases and the choice of employees for promotion stem directly from formal appraisal. With the system exerting that much influence over employees' careers, they will pay close attention. They will listen very carefully to the feedback they receive. And not only will they listen, they will also be strongly motivated to adjust their performances, if necessary, in line with the feedback.

Let's look at the formal system in action. The following anecdote assumes (1) that the managers and employees in King & Barrows both trust the system, and (2) that decisions regarding raises are based on it. Our employee is Jeannine Compton, a secretary at King & Barrows, a pharmaceutical company. She has just emerged from an appraisal session, where her performance has been rated as good, but not outstanding. Her raise will be modest. Jeannine knows that the raise could have been three times or more the percentage she is receiving if she had been rated outstanding. Moreover, she knows in detail why she *isn't* considered outstanding: (1) too many typos in letters submitted for her manager's signature, (2) too many Monday morning absences, and (3) too many personal phone conversations at her desk. She knows that she can correct those three faults. More important, she knows that if she does, and if the improvements are noted in her next appraisal, as they will be, she can increase her income considerably.

This story shows the formal system working smoothly. It *can* work that smoothly, and it will if the proper commitment is made.

Self-appraisal, Peer Appraisal

As a manager, your opinion is the one that counts, but employees can also get information about the quality of their work from other sources. Chief among these are the employees themselves. It's highly likely, for instance, that Jeannine Compton knew she was taking chances with her Monday-morning absences and her personal phone calls. As for the error-filled letters, since her boss was handing them back to her for correction, she had to be aware that she wasn't in the running for Secretary of the Year. She had plenty of self-appraisal data, but it took a formal assessment to stir her to action.

Jeannine is a relatively easy case, as you may have guessed. Employees whose assignments are more ambiguous—the professionals, technical workers, and managers mentioned earlier—are less likely to know how well they are succeeding. Their tasks, being less cut-and-dried, are harder to evaluate. Nevertheless, these people (including you) are almost certain to *try* to assess themselves—it's human nature. And there is persuasive evidence that these self-appraisals are second in importance only to those supplied from above. More about that later.

As you might expect, however, self-appraisals tend to be lenient. Employees generally assess their performances more favorably than their managers do. Even the most self-aware sales rep, or the most honest, can see Reaganesque charisma and bulldog persistence in his performance, whereas his sales manager may see the guy as a glad-hander and a Missouri mule.

The greatest leniency in self-appraisal is almost sure to appear when the results are used to make important decisions about the employees, such as their pay levels. Higher rating—more money. The temptation to be generous is too strong. How could Corporal Sue Swampscott fail to see herself as Field Marshal Susan Swampscott under those circumstances? Because of the risk of leniency in self-assessment, you should avoid it as a source of formal appraisal data.

How about peer appraisal? No. There are built-in problems. Think about it. No matter how high your ideals, could you objectively assess the performance of one of your peers if you knew that a favorable assessment would reduce your own chances for a promotion and a pay raise? That's the glitch. You and your peer are probably vying for the next higher rung on the corporate ladder. And if each year's salary increases come out of a predetermined pool, as they probably do, anyone else's raise automatically decreases yours. In this situation, you would have a hard time praising the contributions of your peer.

What has just been described is exactly what happens when peer or co-worker assessments are used in the formal appraisal process. Everyone looks toward that limited pool of organizational rewards, and idealism sails out the window. Backbiting and infighting begin. Worst of all, perhaps, secrecy sets in, as peers refuse to share relevant information related to their activities. So much for peer input. Avoid it in the formal performance appraisal process.

There's one practice that is even worse, though, and that's asking a manager's subordinates to provide appraisal data on the manager. It's hard to believe that any manager would do it, but there are plenty of tales confirming that it happens. Surely it's apparent that formal appraisals by a manager's subordinates cannot help but undermine the manager's legitimate authority. The manager is supposed to be a leader, not a pincushion. In a worst-case scenario, the manager begins to try to please his or her subordinates rather than maximize the effectiveness of the business unit. It's all but impossible to imagine a situation in which a manager should seek out formal appraisals by subordinates.

Outside versus Inside Expertise

One of the received truths of business is that customer or client satisfaction is of the utmost importance. If it is truly that important to your business unit, and if the employees that you assess play a meaningful role in achieving it, you may want to ask for customer or client input in the appraisal process. You have to be careful what you ask customers or clients to appraise, however. Typically, they can make useful observations only about human relations. They can seldom evaluate an employee's technical competence with any degree of accuracy. So unless you're sure that they have the necessary background, don't rely on customers or clients for technical judgments.

For example, suppose you buy a pearl necklace in a jewelry store. Unless you are a rare customer indeed, you don't know a great deal about the quality of pearls. The salesperson may go into some detail in explaining the lore of pearls to you, but without expertise of your own, you can't really assess his or her product knowledge. What you *can* tell is whether the salesperson was prompt and courteous—and that is all the employee's manager should expect you to assess. Remember, too, that every sales or service job involves performance requirements other than satisfying the customer or client.

In thinking about asking your customers or clients to help out in this way, don't overlook its public relations value. People like to give their opinions on almost anything. They're far more likely to regard your request as an honor than as a burden. And even if you have to discount some of what they say, the PR aspect alone may make it worth your while.

On occasion, you may find that one-time, objective appraisals by external experts are desirable. This is a touchy matter, but there may be no satisfactory alternative if you can't produce a fair and accurate appraisal of the employee yourself. This situation arises most often with employees in technical fields, fields that you don't personally know in detail. An employee may even suggest during an appraisal that you, the manager, are making judgments in the dark. If that happens, an outside appraisal may actually be welcomed.

Vivian Brady, the personnel director of O'Toole, Ltd, felt angry about her performance appraisal. The manager of her business unit hadn't been unpleasant or entirely negative in his appraisal, but he had been (in her view) badly informed. He didn't seem to know much about current personnel practices. Some of his judgments were off base, she felt, because he didn't know the field well enough to make valid assessments. She expressed her unhappiness to the manager, and he frankly admitted that she had some good points.

This seems to be a clear-cut case where appraisal by an outside expert would be useful. The expert would provide a one-time, objective assessment of the personnel director and would also comment on the business unit's appraisal procedures. (Since they didn't work in this instance, procedural changes might well be called for.)

A manager can't possible know the ins and outs of everyone's job. For that reason, outside appraisal can occasionally become a necessity. One business unit manager, for instance, had a nagging doubt about his director of market research. Although he had given the man a number of positive appraisals, he couldn't shake his suspicion that the market research group was providing less help than it ought to be. The manager, having no particular expertise in market research, decided to have an outside expert do the next appraisal. Sure enough, the manager's suspicions were justified. Those earlier positive appraisals of his, based on too little knowledge of market research, had been off base.

Clearly, this practice of using outside experts for conducting formal appraisals can work, sometimes very well. But it should be used only in rare instances. It should emphatically not be used as a routine, recurring procedure. Performance appraisal isn't a responsibility that a manager can delegate on a regular basis.

Top-Down Management

There's no escaping it. The task of appraising an employee's performance falls directly on the shoulders of the employee's manager. As a manager, you usually have the requisite knowledge of what your employees should be doing and how they should be doing it. You are ordinarily in the best position to observe their efforts and the results of those efforts. As a rule, your position gives you enough power to motivate any needed changes in employee behavior.

Finally, since you, as a manager, will be held accountable for your employees' actions, it's only fair that you should be the one to carry out the appraisal and provide the feedback. Part of being a boss is being an evaluator. A manager must be willing to assess the work of others and then lay those assessments on the line. Accept the responsibility. There's no other way to manage smart.

Ten Points to Remember

1. It is important for employees to have feedback about how well management thinks they are performing.
2. Performance appraisals are needed by management as a basis for allocating rewards, identifying training needs, and making sound personnel moves.
3. Any disadvantages of performance appraisals are more than offset by their advantages.
4. Informal assessment of employees can provide desirable support for a formal system of performance appraisals.
5. Formal appraisal at its best is highly accurate; since rewards are tied to performance, it is also very powerful.
6. Self-appraisal has its uses as part of the overall appraisal process, but employees tend to overrate themselves.
7. Peer appraisals and subordinates' appraisals of managers have little or nothing to recommend them.
8. Customers or clients can sometimes provide useful input on the human-relations aspect of your employees' performance.
9. On rare occasions, a one-time, objective performance appraisal by an outside expert may be necessary to achieve fairness.
10. Because managers are accountable for their employees' performance, the smart manager takes full responsibility for appraisals and feedback.

5

Formal Appraisal Systems That Work

P HIL DEVOTO was a middle manager in a small company whose president decided to install time clocks. The president, in a fit of democracy, had decreed that every employee from executive vice president on down the line must have a time card and must punch in and out every day. Loud were the mutterings in the managerial ranks, but what could be done? The Great One had spoken.

Worse was soon to come. The Great One noticed within days that time cards were merely recording, not preventing, late arrivals and early departures. He therefore further decreed that substantial weight would be put on "the tale of the time card," as he called it, at formal evaluation time. Black numbers for on-time employees would be rewarded; red numbers for slugabeds would earn no praise and no raise.

Now, it happened that Phil DeVoto was in the advertising department. He was their in-house superstar when it came to overseeing the creation of direct-mail pieces that attracted buyers the way the Pied Piper attracted rats and children. DeVoto brought in revenue and plenty of it. But, sad to state, he often missed his morning bus. Commuting from the upper west side of Manhattan to the wilds of Bergen County, New Jersey, he tended to arrive anywhere from one to fifteen minutes late. At the other end of the clock, though, he usually stayed at least an hour late and sometimes much more.

You can guess the outcome. The Great One stuck to his guns. "Excuse one, and pretty soon you're excusing them all." The bright morning line of red numbers on DeVoto's time cards was an insult to corporate policy. DeVoto got a dismal rating from his superior, an appropriately shamefaced functionary. DeVoto's spectacular advertising work went for naught. He received no salary increase, not a sawbuck. "We've got to tighten this ship, damn it!"

Well, they had to tighten the ship without Phil DeVoto, who straightaway took a job with a competing firm, an aggressive outfit that now, with better advertising, is cutting deeply into the Great One's market.

Designing the Tools

How could anyone be as purblind as the Great One? Actually, it's all too easy, though the folly is seldom so dramatic.

Performance appraisal systems provide a means of measuring an employee's contributions to the business unit—or at least they are designed to. If an appraisal system specifies the wrong things, if it includes inappropriate performance requirements, or excludes appropriate ones, then management has installed a program that misdirects the efforts of its employees.

Appraisal systems with the wrong requirements are not particularly rare. What seems sensible on the surface may not in fact be sensible. Performance requirements must be carefully and accurately set.

But successful performance appraisal is a complex art. For each performance requirement, there has to be a measurement tool. While managers tend to form overall judgments of an employee, labeling the employee as good or bad, such sweeping evaluations are of little practical use, especially to the employee who wants a genuine assessment. Most employees will adequately meet many of the job requirements, and not so adequately meet others. If the appraisal is to be helpful, the employee has to know in what specific areas he or she is excelling, merely succeeding, just scraping by, or failing.

Somehow there has to be a point-by-point assessment. All these points can later be lumped together for an overall assessment, one that will be useful for certain personnel decisions. But the specific judgments must come first, leading eventually to the general judgment. The opposite approach doesn't work. Appraisal systems that feature only global judgments of employee performance are undesirable. At worst, they resemble the old officer-rating system in the military, where any rating less than "outstanding" could be assumed to mean that the rated officer ("Excellent—and improving!") had been caught in flagrante delicto with the commanding general's daughter, or son, on the parade grounds at high noon.

What design options are available? Broadly speaking, there are two categories of assessment: direct and indirect. Both have advantages. Both have disadvantages.

How to Count Beans

Direct assessment involves counting, counting, counting. It's purely quantitative. You can count the number of units produced or sold, the number of days tardy or absent, the amount of profits generated. The direct approach is very appealing to managers because of its seeming objectivity. Computer-obsessed baseball managers go bananas with this approach, refusing to send a left-handed hitter to bat against a knuckleballing pitcher unless the power alley in right center field is shorter than 387 feet.

Still, the direct approach is often more objective than an indirect method. This sort of assessment does work—*if the counting that's done meshes with stated performance requirements.* If that computer-crazed baseball manager, for instance, was hired to win the pennant (as managers usually are), and his team finishes deep in the cellar, despite gleaming IBM hardware and a Ph.D. statistician, then the highly publicized counting that's done (43 wins, 117 losses) does indeed mesh—or, rather, fail to mesh—with the only stated performance requirement of the poor guy's job (winning the pennant). The manager had better start looking for a third-base coaching job.

The importance of meshing can't be overemphasized. All too often, managers opt for direct methods because of their supposed objectivity, or their ready availability, even though this sort of assessment doesn't fit the requirements of the job to be evaluated.

That was the Great One's mistake. Recall, too, the example of the retail department managers in chapter 3. The managers had virtually no control over their departments' profits. Consequently, there ought to have been no performance requirement for them concerning profitability. No matter how easy it is to measure profitability—and no matter how satisfyingly right it seemed to the CEO to hold those department managers accountable for profits—it made no sense to do so. There has to be a close fit between the job and the measurement. If there isn't, the appraisal is meaningless, and the appraisal system produces irrelevant data.

In brief: Use the direct approach, count those numbers, when reasonable performance requirements mesh with numerical outcomes that are essentially within the employee's own control. Otherwise, no.

Required: Indirect Assessment

A fact of business life is that many, if not most, job requirements demand the use of indirect assessment methods. And it is the indirect approach that gives management the jitters, for understandable reasons. It is far easier to add up sales figures, count the number of widgets coming off the line, or total the number of days late than it is to put your finger on the less tangible factors that make one employee excellent and another so-so.

Yet the change from a manufacturing to a service economy guarantees that indirect assessment will continue to grow in importance. It might be a good idea at this point to clear up a possible misconception. While indirect assessment is the opposite of direct assessment, or number counting, it isn't some sort of subjective mirage. On the contrary, it's quite concrete. It stems from well-defined performance requirements, depends on quantification, and generally produces a numerical rating. The results of indirect assessment will ordinarily appear on paper to be just as clear-cut as evaluations based on direct assessment.

Various types of forms can be used to capture the numerical ratings of indirect assessment. The choice of forms is critical, because the form determines the kind of performance data the system yields. That fact has important implications, because the kind of data available can limit the uses to which the information is put.

Broadly speaking, there are three kinds of indirect appraisal forms: (1) rankings, (2) checklists, and (3) scales. Each of these general categories contains an almost limitless array of choices.

Rankings. Formats for ranking include simple ranking, paired-comparison ranking, and forced-distribution ranking. *Simple ranking* involves merely ranking one's employees from best to worst. It isn't quite as easy as it sounds, though. The ranking should be done within groups of employees sharing the same or similar job titles. It should also be done for each performance requirement of the job, not overall.

Jennifer Semple, executive editor of a technical magazine, uses a simple ranking system. She has four editorial levels on her staff: senior editor, associate editor, assistant editor, and editorial assistant. At each level, each employee has to be ranked against the others at the same level. You can see what would happen otherwise. The senior editors would be ranked best, the associate editors next, and so on. Presumably, in this kind of job especially, the top people are in their positions mainly because they did excellent lower-level work. But even within a level—editorial assistant—it isn't enough to jot down "Ruth Evans first, Dave Greer second," and so on. That's the very type of overall assessment condemned a few pages ago. The editorial assistants have specific performance requirements (eleven of them, to be exact), and Jennifer goes down each of those requirements for each editorial assistant. In doing so, she sometimes finds to her own surprise that some of her earlier, general assessments aren't borne out by the point-by-point evaluations.

These two rules also hold for paired-comparison ranking and forced-distribution ranking.

In *paired-comparison ranking*, the manager (1) forms all possible pairs of employees, (2) ranks the employees within each pair, and (3) converts these paired rankings to obtain a final ranking for each employee. It's rather like a tennis tournament. The final rankings are based on the percentage of times each employee is favored in each possible pair. The paired-comparison system ensures that every employee is evaluated against all other employees in a systematic way.

In *forced-distribution ranking*, you assign a fixed percentage of employees to each of several predetermined levels. In a health-care organization with which the senior author has worked, managers designate the following performance levels:

   I. Outstanding
  II. Very good
 III. Good
  IV. Poor
   V. Unacceptable

Here are the percentage of employees that managers have to assign to each level:

I. 10%

II. 20%

III. 55%

IV. 10%

V. 5%

Thus, a manager ranking twenty employees is forced to distribute them across the five levels as follows:

I. 2

II. 4

III. 11

IV. 2

V. 1

As you can see, this particular system reflects the assumption that most employees are good or better. Different percentages in the various categories could reflect less (or more) optimistic assumptions. In any case, if the designated performance levels in a forced-distribution system correspond to predetermined levels of compensation, the system gives management a highly structured way to make decisions regarding compensation. A fixed number of dollars set aside for raises is awarded in a way that reflects performance.

It sounds great, and it can be. But nothing is perfect. Suppose the company has a small hotshot department side-by-side with a small deadbeat department. That's not an unusual situation. If top management gives the hotshots a much bigger pot to distribute—as it should—the inequities are minimized. Still, if the "worst" performer in the small hotshot department gets no raise, while the "best" performer in the deadbeat department gets a fairly sizable increase, things aren't working out right. That can happen with forced distribution.

It's rather like the old days in New York State when ten Regents Scholarships were awarded to high school seniors in each upstate county. The awards were based on a statewide competitive exam. If you lived in Monroe County (with the City of Rochester) and finished eleventh on the exam, you got nothing. Yet the same exam score that placed you nowhere in Monroe County might easily have placed you first in one of the nearby rural counties: Orleans, Genesee, Livingston. In other words, the score you got—your actual performance—meant less than the county you lived in. That's the problem with forced distribution if it's applied too rigidly and without regard for variables.

Checklist. With a checklist, you typically check off a series of printed items that correctly describe the employee being evaluated. These checked-off items are then converted in one way or another to yield a performance score. The list is often composed of a number of adjectives—cooperative, neat, decisive, considerate, and so on. Because it is so difficult to link general descriptions to specific performance requirements, these adjective checklists are of doubtful value.

On the other hand, the situation is different if a checklist contains precisely stated job behaviors. In that case, the list is a much more desirable appraisal tool. Of course, what really counts is how much time and care have gone into identifying the behavioral items to be included. If the checklist is really good, it can provide you, the manager, with a rich base of descriptive information to convey to employees. You can discuss specific behaviors in some detail rather than merely addressing an employee's general standing in the work group.

Scales. The scale format can be found in many varieties. Most of them don't work very well. The usual appraisal scale asks you to rate an employee's performance on, say, a five-point range from excellent to poor. The difficulty arises because *excellent* means different things to different managers. To one it means "brilliantly exceeding expectations." To another it means "satisfactory." The first manager hands out very few *excellents*; the second manager scatters them around like birdseed. Two employees performing at exactly the same level will get widely disparate ratings from these two managers. That just isn't fair. The appraisal system needs fixing when an employee's job rating is more a function of who the employee's manager is than of the employee's actual performance.

As with checklists, the quickest way out of this dilemma is to design scales that are tied to behaviors rather than semantics. This type of scale is called a Behaviorally Anchored Rating Scale, or BARS. Recent variants on the BARS idea include BOS (Behavioral Observation Scale) and BDS (Behavioral Discrimination Scale). BARS and its variants still use such vague anchors as *excellent*, but they also offer precise descriptions of behavior to define what the points on the scale mean. These descriptions help managers avoid reaching radically different assessments of employees working at the same level. As with any behavior-based tool, it takes time and effort to design satisfactory BARS. Fortunately, industrial psychologists have devised and tested detailed procedures to guide these efforts.

The Smart Manager's System

There is no one best format for indirect assessment. Rankings, checklists, and scales all have their virtues and their drawbacks. No matter what assessment format you use, it must have specific behavioral information on which you can base your appraisal. An overall judgment won't do it. A list of undefined adjectives won't do it.

As you might expect, rankings, checklists, and scales can be used in combination with one another. They are all designed to achieve the same goal—on-target appraisals of employee performance. If you have an accurate and precise set of performance requirements to work with, you can experiment to some extent with these appraisal tools. You can find out which ones work best with which specific performance requirements.

Given the variety of appraisal tools, and the time required to design them, even the smartest manager may decide to seek assistance from a qualified industrial psychologist. Still, the ultimate choices and responsibilities are the manager's.

Timing, or When to Review

Conventional wisdom has it that formal performance appraisals occur once a year. When it comes to evaluating managers, this annual cycle makes sense. Most business units make operational plans on an annual basis. Often these operational plans affect the performance requirements of managers. Ergo, a good case exists for management appraisal sessions that connect with the timing of potential changes in performance requirements.

A case can also be made for more frequent formal appraisals. But in view of the heavy hand of tradition (and, in a practical sense, the costs incurred by more frequent appraisals), the yearly managerial appraisal is probably here to stay.

Not so with appraisals of employees below the managerial level. Here, where performance requirements are relatively constant, formal appraisals should be conducted, and feedback provided, at least twice a year. Although this is a good general rule, it should not be an inflexible one. There are three important exceptions suggested by the pioneering work of Larry Cummings and Don Schwab in their book *Performance in Organizations*.

1. New Employees. During their probationary period, and perhaps longer, new employees should be appraised at least once a month. New employees need reassurance and direction. Managers need data to assist new hires in overcoming any learning difficulties. Moreover, managers need as much data as possible on which to base their decision to retain or not retain a new employee. This retention decision for probationary employees should not be treated as routine.

2. Employees with Performance Problems. Here, too, appraisals should be done at least once a month. These appraisals may focus just on the problem area, or they may be general appraisals. As a rule, the general approach is best, because it helps to keep the employee from channeling too much effort into the problem area, thereby neglecting other, previously satisfactory aspects of the job. Frequent assessment also aids in the monitoring of progress, or, if there is no progress, supplies data on which to base a decision to fire.

3. Employees Being Groomed for Advancement. If you assign developmental job requirements to employees slated for advancement, you should, generally speaking, appraise the performance of those special requirements four times a year. Developmental job requirements prepare individuals for their future assignments and also test promotability. The requirements may include such tasks as completing a course in supervisory skills for a person being groomed for an entry-level management position, or observing and taking notes at a strategy session for a person being prepared for a general management slot. As these developmental requirements are completed, you should formally appraise them and discuss that appraisal with the employee. Assessment of the employee's regular job requirements do not necessarily have to increase in frequency.

No rules regarding the frequency of performance appraisals are cast in bronze. But convention alone should not dictate timing. Instead, such factors as the stability of an employee's performance requirements and the level of his or her performance (or of your expectations concerning promotion) should be taken into account in making decisions about when to appraise.

Lay It on the Line

If new car prices once produced "sticker shock," a formal appraisal session sometimes produces "rating shock." It shouldn't. If there has been adequate informal feedback over the previous twelve months (or however long it is since the last appraisal), the employee should have some inkling of what's coming. Indeed, he or she needs this foreshadowing for your sake, too. Otherwise, you may find yourself dealing with a closed mind during formal feedback. You don't want that at all. You want the employee to be in a receptive frame of mind.

The keynote for the session is honesty. You have to lay it on the line, the bad with the good, the brickbats with the roses.

You have two principal goals when you talk with the assessed employee: (1) *to maintain* performance appraised to be at a satisfactory level, and (2) *to improve* performance appraised at an unsatisfactory level. Both goals—maintaining an employee's steady course and closing any performance gaps—require the same type of feedback session, with one major exception, to be noted later. For now, let's look at five fundamental rules for the session.

Five Rules for the Session

The formal appraisal feedback session is important to the employee, to you, and to the business unit. It should be conducted with a high degree of professionalism.

1. Set the stage. The session should cause the employee to sit up and take notice. Use every possible means to make sure the employee will be primed to listen to what you have to say. For instance:

Tell the employee well in advance where and when the session will take place.

Ask the employee to prepare for the session by doing a thoughtful self-appraisal, either mental or written.

Inform the employee that you will be happy to answer any questions that he or she may have about the appraisal process.

Conduct the session in private, without interruptions.

Avoid small talk; get down to business at the beginning of the session.

2. Give specific details. Just as the appraisal itself should avoid generalities, so should the feedback session. Provide feedback on each performance requirement of the employee's job. Explain in detail why the employee received each specific assessment. Use examples, anecdotes. The employee may or may not agree with your interpretation of events and behaviors, but at least he or she will know what your interpretations are. Generalities, by contrast, make you look weak or uninformed, and even if you make them glowing, they give the employee very little information or confidence.

3. Avoid making character judgments. Employees take appraisals personally. Remember that the employee is under pressure. Remarks that would normally be overlooked can take on exaggerated importance in a formal feedback session. Discuss only performance—only outputs and behaviors. Do *not* comment on what you see as the employee's character—"arrogant," "immature," "moody." Even if you're right, you're wrong. It's essential to explain to the employee the performance data that led you to reach your conclusions. But keep the adjectival judgments to yourself.

Be polite and courteous. Maintain as unemotional an attitude as possible. Don't shout or browbeat. If an employee loses control of his or her emotions, terminate the session gracefully and quickly, and reschedule it at a later date. Don't try to avoid emotions entirely, however. You can't and shouldn't. Your goal is to keep your own emotions and those of the employee from getting out of control. The last thing you want is a feedback session that becomes a subsequent source of embarrassment to either of you.

4. Motivate the employee. No matter what a particular assessment may be, the tone of the session should be constructive. You want to reinforce the desirable aspects of performance and improve the less desirable aspects. That's the basic reason for providing feedback. Give praise where justified. Show displeasure where warranted. And, most of all, indicate the organizational rewards, if any, that the employee's performance has earned. You must show each employee that there is a clear link between appraised performance and rewards such as pay increases and promotions.

5. Formulate an action plan. The four previous rules apply to feedback sessions aimed at maintaining a steady course and at closing a performance gap. The fifth rule deals only with unmet performance requirements. When a performance requirement has not been met, first discuss with the employee the probable cause or causes of the problem. Some causes are obviously beyond the employee's control—a major illness, an office fire. But in the absence of such events, use your combined analysis of the problem as a basis for creating an action plan. Draw up a list of specific steps the employee can take to close the gap. Set up a timetable for each step, and specify when you will review the employee's progress. Both you and the employee must believe that this plan has a good chance of working. Don't try to impose a plan without the employee's agreement—*uncoerced* agreement, that is. Otherwise, your efforts will be wasted, and the employee will feel demoralized. Your aim in devising an action plan is to encourage improved performance. That's *your* aim. But only the employee can implement it.

You'll Need Practice

A formal feedback session requires a certain amount of homework, skill, and practice. You can't just jump in with both feet and pray. You have to be prepared. You have to know quite accurately what you intend to say and how you will say it. You may even want to go over it mentally, or with a friend, before the session. Even so, no matter how good your appraisal tools, no matter how fair and thoughtful your appraisal, no matter how excellent your preparation for the feedback session, you may bomb. Things may not go the way you want them to. Human beings are unpredictable. You may get some startling reactions. You may fail dismally.

But as a smart manager, you won't let one or two failures stand in your way. You will keep on doing the job that needs to be done, and doing it to the best of your ability. With perseverance, you will overcome. As the poet Emily Dickinson put it:

We never know how high we are
Till we are asked to rise
And then if we are true to plan
Our statures touch the skies—

The heroism we recite
Would be a normal thing
Did not ourselves the cubit warp
For fear to be a king—

That truth applies equally well to managers and employees. The second R, review, is a complex, time-consuming, sometimes frustrating process. But when it's done with fairness, integrity, and spirit, it can inspire all personnel from shipping clerk to vice president to strive for the best that is in them.

Ten Points to Remember

1. A good formal performance appraisal, one that is helpful both to employees and to management, provides specific, point-by-point assessment of assigned requirements.
2. Direct assessment involves numerical measures and is effective only if the numbers mesh with stated performance requirements.
3. Indirect assessment yields tangible results, though the measures on which it is based are less concrete than numbers.
4. Performance appraisal forms come in many varieties; the general types are (a) rankings, (b) checklists, and (c) scales.

5. Ranking systems—simple, paired-comparison, and forced-distribution—provide workable ways to rate equal-level employees from best to worst.

6. Performance appraisals of managers are typically made once a year, but employees below the managerial level need to be rated more often.

7. In giving an employee feedback at a formal performance appraisal session, be honest—lay it on the line.

8. A feedback session should rivet the employee's attention, offer specific details, and stick strictly to performance.

9. The tone of feedback sessions should be constructive; you want to improve employee performance, not instill guilt.

10. Devise an action plan to help an employee close the gap between performance requirements and actual performance.

6

How to Reward Performance

I F you were to ask a dozen people at random, "Why do you work?" you would probably see a dozen perplexed expressions. What kind of question is *that?* The answer seems so obvious—"For the money." On the other hand, a bit of reflection will convince you that money isn't the only reason people work.

The question has intrigued researchers for decades. No one knows the whole answer. No one can give you the exact formula of drives and motives that energize, direct, and sustain people on their jobs. Still, we do know *something* about why people work. That knowledge, incomplete as it may be, forms the basis for the recommendations in this chapter.

Herewith the third basic R: rewarding.

Everyone Has to Eat

In order to survive, every animal—including the well-tailored denizen of the executive suite—needs to eat and drink. Psychologically, and sometimes physically, we also need to avoid pain and serious danger. No matter how far most American managers may be from starvation or death by predators, survival is of paramount importance.

The most acceptable way to survive in our society is to work. For the majority of us, the income we gain from work is what pays the rent or mortgage, the grocery bills, the utility bills, the doctors' bills. Without work, there is welfare. Without welfare, even in the most advanced societies, there is a day-to-day struggle for simple survival.

And so we work. On a higher plane, though, we have another kind of motive for working, a motive not shared by the wolves and aardvarks. That motive is our human need to understand, explore, and control our environment. As the last chapter suggested, this need for control is central to the role of work in our lives. We want to see ourselves as competent. We also want to be as free as possible from external restraint. We want personal freedom.

In 1943, Ayn Rand's novel *The Fountainhead* made quite a stir. The hero of the book, an architect presumably modeled on Frank Lloyd Wright, is about as extreme an individualist as you are likely to come across. Nobody, but nobody, orders Howard Roark around. Now, Ayn Rand's hero is scarcely believable. He is the kind of superman you would rather read about than have to put up with. Yet the tremendous success of the book suggests that this desire for individualism, for personal freedom, is a deep-seated wish among most of us.

Personal freedom, whether we like it or not, depends in large part on the amount of money a person earns from work. To be sure, there are a few modern Thoreaus in their bucolic retreats. There are a few people so wealthy that work is an amusement rather than a necessity. But for the rest of us, money provides not only food and shelter but also options.

Pay for What?

Money makes a difference, and the immediate answer to the question "Why do people work?" is basically the right answer. People work for money and for the freedom and satisfaction that money provides. No, money isn't the whole answer, but it's a big part of the answer. A smart manager cannot ignore it or downplay it, because money *is* a primary motivator. Let's look now at how a smart manager uses money wisely.

Managers give pay raises for various reasons, some of them good, some of them not so good. Here are the two main reasons:

1. *Seniority.* If all the old-timers in a company are making more money than any of the newer employees, then seniority is the rule. Loyalty is rewarded; stability is maintained.

2. *Performance.* If raises are based on how well an employee is doing his or her job, the variations in pay will not reflect age or time in service quite so clearly, although there will be some connection.

Other criteria for giving raises are possible. Need is one. Since managers are likely to be aware, at least to some extent, of the financial needs of the people they supervise, this humanitarian element can creep into decisions even when no one intends it to be there. The main reasons for pay raises, however, are seniority and performance. These are exceedingly touchy subjects, as the controversy over teachers' pay in the public schools keeps reminding us.

Two Cheers for Loyalty

Employee turnover costs money. Because of that, it certainly makes sense to reward employees for loyal service. The real question is not whether you should do it, but how much you should pay. Can all raises be based on seniority? The American Federation of Teachers notwithstanding, the answer is no. Good old Lulubelle's thirty-seven years of faithful service with your company are worth something, but not everything.

Only a few percentage points of an employee's base wages should go toward rewarding seniority. If you pay more, there won't be enough left over to reward—and thereby motivate—employee behavior that is much more central to the success of the business than employment stability. The work behavior that needs to be rewarded is job performance. A stable but unproductive work force is deadly.

Perform and Prosper

Pay must be tied to performance. You get what you pay for. That may be a moth-eaten adage, but it is hard to argue with. The writings of such eminent psychologists as Hull, Lewin, Skinner, and Tolman all demonstrate that behavior—any behavior—will be maintained or increased if it is followed by a reward.

Money motivates. But it motivates job performance only when management pays *specifically* for performance. This is a critical point. Words alone won't make a difference. You can tell employees at every coffee break that pay is tied to performance. But they must *see* it. They must know beyond rhetoric and beyond doubt that good performance will in fact earn them more money.

If employees see no close tie between performance and earnings, more money does not lead to better performance. Consequently, it's disheartening to find managers who still hold out against basing an employee's pay on job performance. Why do they do it? For many of the same reasons (discussed in the previous chapter) that they are reluctant to use a formal performance appraisal system. Here, as there, it is a shortsighted policy. An equality rule concerning pay raises can, and often does, lead to unfortunate results.

1. It can maintain unsatisfactory performance levels. Sandra Avery and Joan Bachman have the same job title. They are word-processing operators. Sandra is efficient, conscientious, and productive. Joan is slow, inaccurate, and decidedly marginal. This is no great secret to anyone whose purchase orders they process. Yet when pay-raise time came around recently, they both received the same amount. Joan was delighted. She interpreted her raise as a reward for her performance—that is, slow, inaccurate, and often unacceptable. She snapped her bubblegum proudly and resolved to keep up the bad work.

2. It can lead to turnover among higher-performing employees. Sandra Avery knows perfectly well that Joan Bachman is a klutz. For a year she had been putting up with it and assuming that the obvious differences in performance between her and Joan would be recognized and reflected in their pay raises. Now she knows the truth. "All I have to do on this job is show up at the workstation," she thinks. Now, here's the sad part. The company gave generous pay raises to two employees. Joan, whom they would dearly like to see working for someone else, was pleased. Sandra, whom they appreciate and rely on, soon *will* be working for someone else. Upon learning of Joan's raise, she turned to her word processor and, instead of keyboarding a purchase order, typed in her resume.

This is a case where discrimination is clearly in order. Joan and Sandra's boss doesn't discriminate against her employees on the basis of race, sex, religion, or any criteria of that kind. But she *should* discriminate when it comes to performance. A smart manager strongly advocates the ideals of equal opportunity, but equality of opportunity was not at issue here. Joan had the same opportunity as Sandra to do a good job. But she wasn't doing it, and her boss seemed to be begging to keep a nonperformer on the payroll and lose a good performer to the company down the road.

Then, too, if Sandra does stay, she is less likely to suppose that her own good performance means anything. She will probably continue to do satisfactory work, since that is the nature of conscientious employees, but she will never again have the incentive to go out of her way to help in the hope that it will be recognized and rewarded. She has been effectively demotivated.

What about Group Pay Plans?

Smart managers tie pay raises closely to an employee's job performance. There is an increasing trend today, however, to allocate pay to individuals based on the performance level of their work group. An individual benefits only if the work group as a whole succeeds. Occasionally the work group is the business unit—a division, a company, or a corporation.

This is *not* a desirable trend. An employee can control his or her own performance and no one else's, at least not others' at the same level. Employees understandably see a weaker tie between their performance and their pay under such a plan. The motivational spur of money is a direct one. Sandra Avery, for instance, would hardly want to be teamed with Joan Bachman and then be appraised and paid on the basis of their combined efforts. That is essentially the kind of problem, in less stark terms, that exists with most group pay plans.

These plans are warranted only when the performance levels of individual group members cannot be separated from the total performance of the group. Please don't say right away, "Why, yes, that's the spot I'm in." It rarely is. Even in the case of team sports such as basketball and baseball, where there is a clear-cut group product, a win or a loss, individual contributions to the group can be assessed. And of course they are. Just look at Larry Bird's or Mike Schmidt's salary as against the salary of a promising but unproven rookie.

When group performance is used to measure pay, managers typically have failed to apply the first and second basic Rs. (Look back at Chapter 1 to refresh your memory.) Often, however, managers do not recognize this failure. Instead, they use group pay plans because (1) the need for cooperation within the group is so high and (2) the cost of conflict among members of the group is so great.

These are very real concerns. But the action taken to ensure cooperation, the group pay plan, is flatly wrong. If the need for cooperation is so high, then cooperative behavior should be made a requirement of the individual's job. Cooperation itself becomes a part of performance. The employee is appraised on it. If your employees must help one another, tell them so. Make it mandatory. Evaluate cooperative behavior—and then give rewards for it. Don't take the easy way out and resort to a group pay plan.

If you tie a group pay plan to an entire business unit, the scheme is even less likely to succeed. Since individual control is minimal at the divisional or corporate level, the motivational impact of pay for performance is lower yet. While it's true that performance of the business unit in general has an effect on employee earnings—wages at IBM are higher than at Red Ink Enterprises—that's another matter. The only question here is whether individual pay increases should be based on group performance or business-unit performance, and the answer is no.

The Fair-sharing System

Allocating pay increases to employees is like slicing up a pie. First, obviously, there has to be a pie; and before you think about how generous the slices of the pie ought to be, you must consider the size of the pie itself.

Under the compensation scheme which we'll call fair sharing, the size of the pie is determined by the performance of the business unit. As mentioned earlier, the business unit may be a division, a company, or a corporation. Whatever unit is chosen, it should be as small as possible. The performance of that business unit may then be indexed by profits, return on investment (ROI), or a measure of labor efficiency. It's essential that the indexing be done in strategically relevant terms. You have to be dealing with a real pie, not a mirage. It's equally important that the measure you're using is understood by the employees of the unit.

If a division or company is run as an autonomous unit, with its management held accountable for profits and losses, the unit should have its own fair-sharing plan. It's inequitable not to have one. Take the case of a large bank that based the size of its compensation pie on the corporation's return on investment. Now, this bank has domestic and international units, retail and wholesale units. A few years ago, a single unit—the domestic retail unit—performed so badly that the corporation as a whole ended up with no compensation pie. Merit pay increases were denied to every one of the bank's fifty thousand employees.

As you might guess, employees outside the poor-performing domestic retail unit were outraged. Their units had performed reasonably well but had been dragged down by the one big loser. They felt they had been unfairly treated, and they were right. If each business unit of the bank had had its own fair-sharing plan, only the poor performers would have suffered.

Remember, in choosing business units to have fair-sharing plans, keep the units as small as possible. Big is not better.

Where do you look when you are choosing among profits, ROI, or some other measure on which to base a fair-sharing plan? Look first at the business unit's strategic plan. Ask yourself what performance index will best serve the unit's strategic interests. The answer to this question can vary by industry. For example, in a capital intensive industry—public utilities, let's say—an ROI index is probably more desirable than an index based on labor efficiency. Think carefully about your own business unit's nature and strategy before making a choice.

Once a potential performance index has been chosen, ask yourself, "Can the employees of the unit understand the index, or can they be educated to understand it?" The answer to this question is critical. Although the idea of a compensation pie is simple enough, the way of determining the size of that pie may sound like mumbo-jumbo to many employees. To tell them that ROI will determine how much money is available for pay raises assumes that they know what ROI is and what factors influence it. They may not know. You'd better tell them. If the employees know that the pie is genuine, that its size is based on reality and not on whim, and that their own collective efforts can truly expand or shrink the pie, your fair-sharing plan will be off on the right foot.

Deciding What's Fair

Fairness is a tough concept to pin down, yet it is much talked about. You'll remember that in the 1984 presidential campaign, Walter Mondale's advisers urged him to push the "fairness issue." Fairness, like motherhood, is much admired. It is often a topic of political and legal discussion.

Business has to be concerned with fairness, too. And it isn't easy, not even with a good fair-sharing plan in place. Let's take an example. A business unit has been defined and a performance index chosen. Now all that remains is to decide the precise relationship between the performance index and the size of the pie. The task is far from simple. For example, we'll say that profits have been chosen as the best performance index for a particular business unit. Last year was a good one; profits increased 20 percent. The question is this: What share of those profits should be allocated for increases in employee compensation?

The answer is this: There is no answer. Nobody has a pat solution. Like Smilin' Jack of old, you're flying by the seat of your pants in this area. Yet there is a vague but cardinal rule to be followed. It may sound like one based on circular reasoning, but here it is: The size of the compensation pie should be *fair*. This requires honest and open discussions between management and employees of the business unit, with both relying on facts to resolve any disagreements.

It's much easier to identify instances of unfairness than of fairness. You probably can cite some instances from your own experience. A well-publicized example occurred in the early 1980s when many public transportation companies were losing money. There was simply no pie to be sliced. The management of some of these companies asked employees to take sizable pay cuts. So far, so good. All employees of a business unit should share in the unit's losses as well as in its gains. However, the managers did not take pay cuts themselves. Their salaries remained untouched—a clear-cut case of unfairness that would, and did, appall a great many people.

Gross unfairness is easy to spot, but what about fairness? Deciding how to assess a fair share is a tough matter in most businesses. It's a problem that has puzzled management for a long time and is likely to continue challenging it.

The challenge cannot be dismissed. It has to be faced, and faced now. Our nation's economic vitality may depend on it. One survey after another has shown that American workers know they could be more productive, but refuse to be. Why? Partly because they don't believe that their increased productivity will be rewarded. And in too many cases they are right. Explicit financial incentives do not really exist in many companies to reward improved performance.

Fair-sharing plans, no matter how crude, will go a long way toward restoring the work ethic to corporate America. Compare big businesses with small businesses. Individual entrepreneurs (those in Silicon Valley, to take a notable example) often work nights, Sundays, and holidays, not because they are unimaginative grinds but just the opposite—because they know that their efforts will be directly rewarded. The same thing must happen in large businesses. Managers cannot expect people to put forth their maximum effort without knowing that they will be justly rewarded. The concept of *just reward* is a basic principle on which our economy has flourished, a principle too many corporations have too long ignored.

Four Aspects of Fairness

A few pages back, seniority was mentioned and then shunted aside as performance took the forefront. But we can't forget seniority. Nor can we forget another factor not mentioned before—the employee's job title. In all business units, compensation levels are tied to job titles. Because of labor market forces, different jobs pay different amounts of money. Secretaries, as a group, don't make as much as engineers. Custodians, as a group, don't make as much as personnel directors. This may be elementary, but it can't be ignored. The secretary who gets a 7 percent pay increase will quickly turn to her calculator and discover the next year's pay will be $980 higher than this year's. She'll also know that the same percentage increase applied to her boss's salary will add up to a $5,040 raise. Is *that* fair? It may be, depending on a number of factors, including competitive pressures in the external labor market. That may be a heavy concept to lay on a twenty-year-old secretary, but it's a fact of business life.

In any case, the absolute amount of merit increase allocated to a particular employee will be based on four criteria:

1. The performance of the business unit
2. The employee's job title
3. The employee's seniority

4. *Most important*, the employee's assessed individual job performance

William H. Whyte, Jr., a *Fortune Magazine* editor in the 1950s, wrote an article in which he suggested that a clever business speaker should reverse the old conference-table cliché, attracting attention with the statement, "Gentlemen, I have a panacea." It may seem that fair sharing is being offered as a panacea. After all, fair sharing motivates performance; it helps shift voluntary turnover to low-performing employees; and it gives all employees a sense that they share a common fate with the business unit.

Pretty good. In fact, so good that the last point deserves elaboration. All too often, employees have a "we–they" attitude toward management, with the managerial they being viewed as an adversary. Under fair sharing, a "we–they" relationship also exists, but the identity of the they changes. It becomes the business unit's competition, along with other forces that hinder progress or impede success. Fair sharing creates a sense of shared purpose, which pays off in employee commitment to the business unit. It results in a willingness on the part of employees to work hard, to stick with the unit through difficult as well as prosperous times, and to identify with the unit's business goals.

So perhaps it *is* a panacea. Perhaps. But other conditions have to be met before an optimal level of commitment can be reached. Stay tuned.

Ten Points to Remember

1. Money is a powerful motivator when it is fairly and properly apportioned.
2. Seniority indicates loyalty, which deserves some financial reward—but only a fraction of the reward.
3. Pay should be tied to performance, and employees should realize beyond the shadow of a doubt that it *is* tied to performance.
4. Failure to tie pay to performance can reinforce poor work habits and demotivate better-performing workers.
5. Group pay plans are not a good idea, because an employee cannot control the performance of others at the same level.

6. If cooperation is vital on a particular job, make it a stated and assessed requirement of the job.

7. Under fair sharing, the size of the compensation pie should be determined by the performance of the smallest feasible business unit.

8. In choosing a performance index for fair sharing, look to your business unit's strategic plan.

9. An employee's job title, like seniority, is one of the factors involved in determining pay raises.

10. Fair sharing creates a sense of common purpose in the business unit, eliminating the counterproductive we–they attitude between employees and managers.

7

Fair-sharing Techniques

THE pie is on the table, and all the Eastern Region sales representatives gather round. There's Tommy Starr, who led the
group in total sales and in percentage of increase over the previous
year. There's Jackie Flatt, who plugs along at the same satisfactory
but unspectacular level every year. There's Evelyn Pitts, who missed
her sales quota by a country mile, sells cosmetics on the side, and
leads the group in frequency of customer complaints.

And there are many more reps around the table, each one wanting
a generous slice of that enticing pie. What to do?

Getting Down to Cases

Tommy Starr has been with the company two years, Jackie Flatt
seven years, and Evelyn Pitts twelve years. Evelyn suggests that seniority would be an ideal way to cut the pie. Well, you know better
than that, and so, no doubt, does she.

The right way to do it, as you also know, is to award the largest
slice of the pie to the sales rep who has best fulfilled the requirements
of his or her job. Clearly, that's Tommy Starr. But just how much
should Starr get? And how much more than the others?

The answer has to start not with Tommy Starr but at the other
end of the scale, with Evelyn Pitts. What kind of increase should she
get? The answer is simple: None. She has failed to meet the minimal
requirements of the job. Remember, the size of the slice is to be
based on performance, not on seniority. Payment for performance—
a merit increase—demands that the raise be earned. Unacceptable

performance doesn't dictate a modest increase; it dictates *no* increase. This is a tough call. It has to be. Any pay increase given to Evelyn Pitts would be unfair, because it would reward failure. It would take money away from deserving sales reps who did perform well.

Let's say you are using a forced-distribution ranking system for your performance appraisals. You assign all employees with the same or similar job requirements to one of five performance levels. Your own assessment puts them there. Once they are there, what can they expect in the way of pay increases? The following table gives a graphic answer.

Performance Level	Percentage of Employees	Compensation
I. Outstanding	10	$********
II. Very good	20	****
III. Good	55	**
IV. Poor	10	*
V. Unacceptable	5	0

The cash value of * can be mathematically determined by the size of the pool and the number of employees who are to share in it. The important thing to consider in the example is not the likely dollar amounts but rather the geometry of the chart. According to the asterisks, an outstanding performer (Tommy Starr) will get an increase that is four times larger than that of an average performer (Jackie Flatt). Is that fair? Yes, it is.

To motivate employees, there has to be a meaningful difference in compensation between the different performance levels. A good rule of thumb is to double the amount of the increase from the good to the very good rating and to double it again for an outstanding rating. You may prefer other figures, but the basic principle should apply: The differences in compensation between performance levels must be significant—and your employees must see them as significant.

What about Bonuses?

The preceding talk of compensation, pay raises, and merit increases may have led you to think that only base salary is being discussed.

That isn't the case. A merit increase can take different forms. And, as a matter of fact, an increase in the employees' base pay may not be (and probably isn't) the best option.

Here's why. When you raise an employee's base salary based on performance over the last six months or a year, you are building that increase into the employee's salary for as long as he or she stays on the payroll. That isn't fair to the business unit. Six months' performance should not confer lifetime benefits. Base wages should be raised for other reasons—a change in job title, competitive labor market pressures, or seniority—but not for short-term performance.

What is the alternative? One good choice is the one-time cash bonus. In fact, any option is worth considering if it doesn't involve a regularly recurring expenditure and doesn't cost more than a good bonus plan. As a rule, organizations devise imaginative and appealing compensation plans for senior management. A little of the same creativity applied for the benefit of the rest of the employees can have equally positive effects.

For example, why not let employees apply their bonus dollars to a wide choice of optional fringe benefits? Although TRW and American Can don't operate under a fair-sharing system, both offer their employees a choice of fringe benefits. Offering choices in this way increases the motivational impact of the incentive dollars.

Another excellent way to pay for performance is to offer the option of ownership—a piece of the action. Most employees understand, or can be taught to understand, the concept of equity capital. Nothing creates a sense of shared purpose more effectively than being a stockholder in one's company. Over the next few years there is likely to be a radical increase in stocks being offered, not just to senior management but to all employees, as an optional form of payment for their performance.

Appraisal, Then Payment

Managers differ in their views on when to pay out merit dollars, yet there's a rule of thumb that seems to apply. Your employees, with the exceptions noted earlier, probably receive formal performance appraisals every six months or twelve months. If so, it makes sense to tie cash bonuses or other incentives to those ratings, not only in dollars but also in time. As every teacher knows, rewards deferred are rewards diluted. You want employees to see clearly and quickly the cash value of their performance.

Payment for certain kinds of incentives—various fringe benefit options, for example—require a yearly schedule. Some employees, such as salespersons working on a commission basis, need to be rewarded more frequently than every six months. The guiding principle is this: To motivate performance, reward it promptly, and tie the reward to the performance with strong, visible twine.

If the Union Objects . . .

Will the union, if there is a union, object to fair sharing? Probably. Organized labor has a long history of opposing merit compensation. This opposition is rooted in the belief that management cannot accurately, fairly, or even defensibly appraise employee performance in a way that justifies tying compensation to it. You will ignore this objection at your peril. More realistically, you will be unable to ignore it, and perhaps you will be unable to overcome it.

Look at it from the union's viewpoint. The union can persuasively argue that corporate management, even in the best-run companies, is far from saintly. People are human, no matter how exalted their titles or how awesome their power. Old-boy politics exist almost everywhere, and they influence business decisions; old-girl politics loom on the horizon. Off-the-wall promotions of personnel are legion. Gloria Steinem did not invent sexual politics.

Corporate hierarchies, the union will maintain, seldom give much comfort to observers who trust that the best and the brightest finish first. Leo Durocher was right, wasn't he?—the good guys (or gals) finish last, not first. Back-scratching and brownnosing and bubble-headed individual judgments are too glaring in many companies to be denied. To suppose that uniformly fair rankings within a business unit can be reliably obtained, via indirect appraisal, is to suppose what is not and has never been.

Cynical? Yes, but too often true. The lack of trust, stemming from a well-placed belief in human frailty, has to be countered if fair sharing is to have a chance. Any workable solution must attack that lack of trust. Lavish assurances won't do it. Words, however nicely chosen, won't work. Only action will do it. Somehow the union has to see—and *believe*—that a fair-sharing system *is* fair and is truly working, or is going to work, in the employees' best interests.

The fair-sharing system must be developed slowly. It must have the support, however grudging, of union representatives. Then, when the plan is in place, you, the manager, must be honest. You must provide employees with enough information (some of which may have been privileged in the past) to show what is being attempted. This may involve lengthy discussions with union representatives and groups of employees. You may have to discuss historical successes and failures within the business unit. You may have to touch on strategic planning.

Certainly, you will have to lay the fair-sharing plan on the line. You will have to talk about expected performance levels, explain why the proposed compensation has been tied to each level, and indicate how an employee's appraised performance leads to an assigned level. Secrecy will get you nowhere. Concealment and fair-sharing plans don't mix. The union, hostile or not, has to give fair sharing a fair chance, and it won't give it if the union representatives think you have a stiletto hidden in your vest or an ace up your sleeve.

Fair sharing is not a gimmick. Performance on the job must be rewarded. Otherwise, the business unit's compensation dollars are being tossed out the window. What should be incentives cannot be treated as entitlements. Crassly put, you can buy, within definable limits, better performance from your employees. And you should.

A final note: Fair sharing is not a profit-sharing plan like IMPRO-SHARE, the Scanlon Plan, the Rucker Plan, or any of the others in the same genre. It does, like them, base the share of the compensation pie on some index of business-unit performance. But it goes one step farther. A critical step. It insists that the pie be cut according to individual, not collective, performance levels. A team is a team, yes, but a superstar is worth eight utility infielders.

Final Thoughts on Money

This chapter has put a lot of emphasis on money. That isn't because money is the sole motivator of human behavior, but because money *is* a motivator and is so often used in ways that are nonmotivational. Fair sharing should be used along with other techniques to promote desired levels of performance. After money, two of the best and most familiar motivators are praise and changes in job titles. Let's look at each of them.

The Power of Praise

Newspaper columns on business are rife with letters from readers that go something like this: "How can we get our boss to tell us when we do a good job? We work hard and usually meet our production quotas without overtime, but the only time we get any attention is when we foul up."

It's an old complaint. Paul Black, a market-research executive, still recalls the day in high school when, as a graduating senior, he wanted to get a letter of recommendation for college from his principal. Although there were fewer than two hundred students in the graduating class, and although Paul was to be valedictorian, the principal didn't know him from Kamala, the Ugandan Giant. The kids the principal knew and greeted by name were the misfits, the screw-ups, the reformatory-bound burnouts who came to his attention on an almost daily basis. Understandable, but unfortunate.

A little deserved praise would have done Paul and the letter writers a world of good. Since recognition for a job well done can be a powerful motivator, you should make optimum use of this cost-free method of rewarding performance. Employees want praise and feel they deserve it, yet you, as a manager, will seldom learn that directly from an employee. People tend to mutter among themselves about the lack of praise from on high, or else not to express it at all.

If praise is to be effective, it has to come from a manager the employee respects. And it has to be sincere. Any time you overpraise performance, or any time you bestow praise indiscriminately, you lessen your credibility and reduce the motivational force of the praise. Praise, like money, has to be rationed to some extent, and it has to be apportioned fairly.

You may already use one or more methods of formal recognition for outstanding performance: letters of commendation, plaques, trophies, newsletter articles. Such programs are desirable so long as the recognition is based on validly assessed performance.

Herewith an example of how not to do it: Derek Regis was a sales representative in east Texas for a major textbook publisher. Every elementary school in his sales territory was choosing one elementary math series out of the five series on the approved list for purchase. The amount of sales time available for presenting the series to individual schools was severely limited, as always in Texas book adoptions. Derek's company had high hopes for substantial sales in east Texas. The series had received the highest of the five top ratings from the state evaluators.

Into east Texas poured an army of company personnel—sales reps from nearby states, product managers and editors from the home office—all intent on selling the series. They did. It swept the field. As a consequence, Derek Regis received the largest cash bonus in company history (since all sales in his territory were credited to him, regardless of who had actually made them). Now, this caused some grumbling in the home office—no one there had made an extra dime—but it was nothing compared to what came next.

The company had an Employee of the Year award, which itself featured a sizable amount of cash to accompany the trophy. Having just tripled his base salary on the efforts of that ad hoc Texas team, Derek Regis now jetted into the home office to accept his Employee of the Year award. The Math Editorial Department was incensed. After all, how had their series achieved the highest ranking in Texas except through editorial excellence? Product Marketing was in a twit. All their efforts toward selling another department's product had succeeded wildly, brought them not a sou, and now a lucky beneficiary of their higher-level expertise was walking off with a double prize. The sales reps from neighboring states were crying in their beer. While their territories were being briefly ignored during the big Texas push, and their own bonuses correspondingly reduced, Derek Regis, the one guy who had merely done his job, was waxing fat.

The formal announcement of the award in the company cafeteria brought a chorus of boos. Not a good way to motivate the troops.

Job Title Changes

Typically, a change in job title involves a promotion with an accompanying raise in pay. Promotions based *solely* on performance, however, can be dangerous. Candidates for promotion need to be assessed in terms of their potential for the job to which they will be evaluated. Past success in a different job is not usually a sufficient indicator.

Lateral moves can sometimes be made as rewards for performance, too. A lateral move may put the designated employee in a job that he or she sees as more satisfying. The job may offer more variety or autonomy, even though it isn't a step up the corporate ladder. Frequently, lateral moves serve another purpose as well. They groom the employee for a subsequent move that is in fact a promotion. Of course, the employee must *want* to make the lateral move if it is to be used as a reward for performance.

The Smart Manager's Mission

You have now covered the three basic Rs of managing people: requiring, reviewing, and rewarding. The three are intertwined. If you don't specifically require, you can't sensibly review. If you don't accurately review, you can't fairly reward. In the words of the popular song, "You can't have one without the other."

In applying the three Rs, your goal isn't merely to follow all the steps, challenging as that may be. Your goal is to build an ever stronger business unit. The three Rs are crucial to that goal, as are a few other related topics. One of them is effective hiring, which comes next.

Ten Points to Remember

1. Since pay for performance is the essence of fair sharing, unacceptable performance brings *no* pay increase.
2. Under fair sharing, an outstanding performer should receive a substantially larger increase than an average performer; four times more is a reasonable average.
3. To motivate employees, the differences in compensation between different performance levels must be significant enough to make employees notice.
4. A merit increase should not usually be an increase in base pay; a cash bonus or some other one-time reward is fairer.
5. Letting employees choose from a number of optional fringe benefits is a good way to let them use bonus dollars.

6. To motivate performance, incentive payments should accompany performance appraisals, or follow them as soon as possible.

7. If a union is involved in implementing fair sharing, you will have to make it absolutely clear that the system is fair and will be beneficial to its members.

8. Well-deserved praise can be a powerful, cost-free motivator.

9. Job title changes can be motivational; even lateral moves can sometimes serve the purpose.

10. The three Rs, properly applied, will help you achieve your overall goal—building a stronger business unit.

8

Steps to Better Hiring

SOME years ago there was a best-selling book called *Do You Sincerely Want to Be Rich?* If it weren't for the word *sincerely*, it would be just another book title, but with *sincerely* there are any number of implied questions. Have you been kidding yourself about wanting to be rich? Do you have any ambition? Do you have any perseverance? Or are you just a dreamer, pinning your hopes on the Atlantic City slot machines or the Pick Six lottery?

The basic question in this chapter raises similar issues: "Do you sincerely respect your employees?" If you find yourself hedging on the answer, you may be ignoring a problem that needs solving, avoiding action that needs taking. Respecting your employees, holding them in high regard, is crucial to managing smart. And the truth is that many managers don't respect their employees.

The Fourth R Again

If you, as a manager, don't respect a few, some, or many of your employees, you undoubtedly know why. Either you or your predecessor has failed to choose employees who have earned your respect. Or else you (or managers before you) have failed to develop their potential so that they *can* be respected. Two essentials, then, of the fourth R, respect, are (1) choosing employees you are likely to respect, and (2) developing, or training, employees so that they can be respected. This chapter and the next two deal with these vital issues.

Advantages of Full Disclosure

As a manager, you may see the hiring process as more one-sided than it really is. You need a person to fill a position. You need the right person, someone who can do the job for you. That's accurate enough, as far as it goes. But prospective employees are looking for something, too. They have to decide whether they can meet your expectations. They have to judge whether they will get an adequate level of satisfaction from working with you. People want to do a good job and be happy doing it.

In other words, hiring is a two-way street—or maybe a two-edged sword is a better metaphor. Hiring is tricky. It can't be done blindly. In fact, it should be done with the most and best information you can obtain about a prospective employee.

It works the other way, too. Full disclosure of the requirements of the job will allow a candidate to assess realistically the chances of meeting those requirements. A candidate who sees a poor fit probably won't accept an offer. People don't want to fail. They don't want to put themselves into a situation where they think they will fail.

Not only does full disclosure help people select themselves out of positions in which they doubt their ability to perform, it also "inoculates" the successful applicant, to use the words of Dr. John Wanous of Ohio State University, against future disappointments on the job. It thereby reduces employee turnover. When new hires quit their jobs early on, it is usually because their expectations haven't been met. And their expectations haven't been met, in many cases, because of a lack of full disclosure during the hiring process.

Think about it. When you interview a prospective employee, do you present your business unit in glowing terms? Do you make the job sound more attractive than it is? There is a natural tendency to be positive. You don't want to knock the organization. You don't want to denigrate the job. You don't want the person who is offered the job to turn it down.

Unfortunately, this advertising-brochure approach to interviewing can create unreasonable expectations. (New Hire: "You told me I would get a big raise in six months." Old Boss: "No, I told you there was a possibility of some sort of raise after six months. Actually, the only person who ever got one was Flo Swift back in '72. She's now manager of our Chicago office.") An employee who has been led to expect more than you are in fact prepared to offer is going to be disappointed, perhaps disappointed enough to leave.

You might think that full disclosure would reduce the likelihood of a candidate accepting a job offer. According to the research evidence reviewed by Dr. Wanous, however, that doesn't happen. People are favorably impressed by candor in the recruiting process. In general, they will accept a fully described job (if they think they can handle it) even when the minuses are laid side by side with the pluses.

Knowing What You Want

The person you hire has to be able to meet the job requirements. You know those requirements. Indeed, you *have* to know them if you hope to select the right person. You have to know the mix of skills and abilities you are seeking.

This means that thoughtful application of the first R, requiring, will go a long way toward identifying your new employee. But knowing the specific requirements is not enough. You also need a procedure to follow. One such procedure is known as *job analysis*.

In his book *Staffing Organizations*, Dr. Benjamin Schneider of the University of Maryland defines job analysis as a method "for describing the demands jobs make on people—for describing what the job requires in terms of individual attributes." Several types of job analyses are available. One is the U.S. Department of Labor's *Handbook for Analyzing Jobs*, which rates a job according to individual attributes that are likely to be demanded from a person holding that job. The listed attributes include aptitudes, temperaments, interests, physical capabilities, and so on. Under aptitudes, for example, you will find the following:

Intelligence

Verbal

Numerical

Spatial

Form perception

Clerical perception

Motor coordination

Finger dexterity

Manual dexterity

Eye–hand–foot coordination

Color discrimination

The Department of Labor has gone one step farther, publishing an invaluable book called *Dictionary of Occupational Titles*. This book categorizes over thirty thousand jobs according to the attributes required. You can turn to the *Dictionary* to help you specify the particular skills and abilities you want a new employee to have. As you might suppose, effective use of the *Dictionary* requires that you have established precise job requirements for the position you plan to fill.

The Department of Labor's job analysis procedure is by no means the only one available. You will want to look into some of them, if you haven't already done so. Unless you know the skills and abilities necessary to meet the requirements of the vacant job, your chances of selecting Mr. or Ms. Right for it are practically nil.

The Search for Mr. or Ms. Right

Once you know what skills and abilities you are looking for, you are ready to generate a pool of job applicants from which to choose. This can be done in various ways. Dr. John Wanous's research shows that the best way is through referrals from present employees. By *best* he means applicants who are qualified for the job *and* who, if chosen, are likely to remain on the job for a long time.

But what if you don't respect your present employees and don't trust their judgment? Or what if your employees aren't motivated or willing to make referrals? The evidence suggests that self-initiated referrals are the next best bet.

There are two kinds of self-initiated referrals. The first come from former employees, the second from so-called walk-ins. Walk-ins may be people who write to inquire about employment or people who come in off the street and fill out an application form. In a large business, they may be employees in another department or facility who learn about the open position through word of mouth or a bulletin-board posting.

Any of the foregoing methods are better than relying on newspaper ads or employment agencies.

When you begin to recruit, think long and hard about your recruiting strategy. The pool of applicants you generate will determine the quality of person you hire. That's an ironclad law. If you haven't gotten an application from the best person or persons for the job, you won't be hiring the ideal candidate.

An effective recruiting strategy is analogous to a good marketing plan. Indeed, you might want to consider using in-house marketing expertise in devising a strategy that will attract prime applicants.

Making the Most of Interviews

The interview is an important tool of hiring, but before you embrace it too hastily, step back for a moment and examine it. The interview is an excellent way to inform candidates about the business and about the specific job they are seeking. It is also a good way to obtain factual and biographical information about a candidate. However, to base a selection decision solely on an employment interview is foolhardy.

Why is it foolhardy? Because talking with someone for a limited amount of time on a variety of subjects cannot yield enough data to warrant a decision about that person's suitability or likely performance. Furthermore, it is well known that interviewers' judgments can be, and often are, based on matters irrelevant to performance. An interviewer tends to form assessments very, very early in the interview. A candidate who gets off to a bad start creates an initial but permanent handicap for himself or herself. Finally, many first impressions are based on a candidate's appearance, voice, or personal mannerisms. For many jobs, those factors are irrelevant.

The interview as a selection tool, then, must be approached warily. It can work in some instances. When the interviewing process is highly structured, and when the interviewer is thoroughly trained in the process, it becomes somewhat safer to rely on assessments made during interviews. Safer, but far from safe. The employment interview works best as a technique for sharing and collecting information, not as a vehicle for decision making.

A BIB for Grown-ups

An alternative to the interview as a decision-making vehicle is the written interview, or *Biographical Information Blank* (BIB). A BIB is a questionnaire requesting information about the personal history of the candidate. Essentially, it asks about the candidate's past successes and failures. Its design and use are predicated on the idea that the best way to predict future behavior (performance on the job) is to look at past behavior (personal history).

And it seems to work. Research shows that if BIBs are carefully designed and evaluated, they are a reliable method for making selection decisions. They aren't used very often, however. People evidently have more faith in information collected in a face-to-face encounter (with all its pitfalls) than in a more objective paper-and-pencil procedure (with its apparent record of success).

Exceptions do exist. For many years, the life insurance industry has selected salespersons by means of a BIB (called the AIB) designed and scored by the Life Insurance Marketing and Research Association. This AIB provides a model that is well worth emulating.

How to Choose and Use Aptitude Tests

An aptitude test attempts to assess a candidate's *potential* for demonstrating desired skills and abilities. You should seriously consider using aptitude tests for openings where substantial on-the-job training will be required. After all, you can't make any direct assessment under these circumstances. You *know* the applicant can't do the job yet. The fundamental question is, can he or she learn to do it? And that is precisely what an appropriate aptitude test can answer.

Never mind the bad publicity surrounding the Scholastic Aptitude Test (SAT). Most of the persistent SAT criticism has nothing to do with this test's predictive record—its scores correlate very well with actual college performance, which is what they are supposed to correlate with. The criticism is directed rather at the societal causes and effects of SAT scores. The argument is a legitimate one, and there are strong advocates on both sides, but the controversy has little to do with the validity of this or any other aptitude test. Good aptitude tests work.

Nevertheless, they have to be carefully chosen. You must be convinced of their ability to predict, reliably and accurately, a person's actual performance in subsequent training or on the job. You need a test that has been proved in use, one that has the demonstrated ability to do what you want it to do. Thus, if a job requires an employee to perform mathematical computations, you will want a standardized test that assesses mathematical aptitude. If you choose the test well, you will have a sound selection tool.

Literally hundreds, perhaps thousands, of aptitude tests are on the market. Caveat emptor, with a vengeance. These tests vary widely in intent, quality, usefulness, and price.

Among the better-known multiaptitude tests is the *General Aptitude Test Battery* (GATB). The GATB is designed to gauge the following aptitudes:

Verbal

Numerical

Spatial

Form perception

Clerical perception

Motor coordination

Finger dexterity

Manual dexterity

General intelligence

You will notice that this list is very similar to the Department of Labor's list of aptitudes in its job analysis procedure. What this similarity shows is how neatly a job analysis may mesh with available aptitude tests, permitting you to collect data on which an accurate selection decision can be based.

Again, though, let the buyer beware. Before purchasing an aptitude test, have it reviewed by an expert to make sure the test has been designed and evaluated in accordance with scientific principles. You don't want to buy a product that has limited potential for yielding the type and quality of information you need. Just like the flaky guys down on Sepulveda selling low-mileage cream puffs, the marketers of aptitude tests are out to sell a product, and what they say has to be viewed with a saltcellar of skepticism.

Achievement and Work-sample Tests

Of the three methods available to assess the fit between desired skills and abilities and the attributes a job applicant actually has—interviews, aptitude tests, achievement tests—a strong case can be made that achievement tests are the most reliable. These tests don't measure potential; they measure what a person can actually do. Aptitude tests are predictors, but achievement tests are (or should be) immediate and direct indicators.

One type of achievement test that helps to make the case for them is the work-sample test. This test requires candidates to do the kind of work—a standardized sample of work—that comprises an important aspect of the job for which they are being considered. Candidates are then systematically evaluated on how well they did on the sample. The evaluations translate into scores that can be used as the basis for a selection decision.

Many such tests exist. Candidates for a typing job are asked to type. Candidates for a stockbroker's job at one large financial-services firm are asked to telephone prospects (role-playing prospects, of course) to sell them financial instruments. Candidates for a faculty job at the senior author's university are asked to conduct a seminar. These three examples indicate why achievement tests can be so useful. There is a direct connection between the test and the actual work.

A brief word about so-called motivation tests. These tests, including various personality and interest tests, purportedly can be used to predict how hard a candidate will work at the job for which he or she is being considered. According to the available evidence, this simply isn't so. No test has yet been developed that can predict motivation with any degree of reliability or accuracy. Some managers seem to be highly attracted to motivation tests as selection tools. Don't be. Until test making has progressed well beyond its present limits, the smart manager will steer clear of motivation tests during the selection process.

Four Questions to Ask

You will often find yourself with several kinds of information on a number of candidates for a position. What do you do? Industrial psychologists have developed procedures for statistically combining assessments of candidates to aid you in making a choice. In the final analysis, however, the choice is yours. Ask yourself these four questions:

1. Have I precisely determined the skills and abilities required of job applicants for the open position?
2. Have I thoughtfully generated an appropriate pool of job applicants for the vacancy?
3. Have I reliably and accurately assessed the fit between required skills and abilities and those actually possessed by each job applicant?
4. Have I systematically combined the information available to me and used it to make my selection?

As a smart manager, you should be able to answer yes to each of these questions. But to do so with confidence, you may have to seek advice, counsel, and training. If so, do so. Your efforts will probably prove costly and time-consuming, but they are the best means you have of assuring yourself of hiring employees who are likely to earn your respect.

Hiring from Within

So far the discussion has dealt with hiring employees new to the business unit. All of the procedures described, however, can also be used when choosing from among your unit's current employees. It is an excellent idea to recruit your own employees to fill job vacancies. As noted earlier, job transfers and promotions can be highly effective motivators. An immediate plus is that you ordinarily have more and better information on current employees than you are likely to get on outsiders. Generally speaking, it makes sense to look inside before going outside, unless your specific aim is to bring someone in to play the role of change agent.

One warning: Don't play the games that some companies play with internal postings of already-filled job openings. Nothing is more irritating to an employee than to apply for an open position where none in fact exists. Pro forma postings, required by company policy or worries about equal employment opportunity (EEO), are serious demotivators if employees begin to view them as fictitious. When some, or even most, of the posted jobs have already been filled, a conscientious employee's hope of advancement via that route soon sours. Such postings, which are more in the nature of imaginary employer obligations than of real employee opportunities, are pointless at best and almost certainly unnecessary.

With an Eye toward Promotion

Sometimes your aim in hiring is not merely to fill an immediate position but also to provide for filling future openings. This happens most often when there is an explicit plan for hiring new employees and then moving them up a career ladder to a targeted job.

For example, the strategic plan of a retailing firm calls for the opening of quite a few new stores in each of the next five years. Each store will need a store manager, a position that requires experience. Over time, the firm has determined that a successful store manager needs to work six months as a department manager and then twelve months as an assistant store manager. Looking to the future, the firm sees that it cannot create enough store managers by merely promoting current employees. It needs to hire new people whose skills and abilities match the requirements of all three jobs: department manager (entry level); assistant store manager (first promotion); and store manager (second promotion).

Recruitment and selection are decidedly more complex in a situation like this, but all the same principles apply. Indeed, their use is doubly (or triply) important because an unusual commitment is being made. Most new hires cannot confidently expect two rather rapid promotions. These beginning department managers can.

Did You Make the Right Choice?

Anyone who makes decisions will make mistakes. No matter how carefully you recruit and select new employees, you will sometimes reject qualified candidates and sometimes hire people who later fail to meet minimum job requirements. By applying the concepts presented in this chapter, you will reduce the number of errors, but you will not totally eliminate them.

Recognizing the errors you do make is of paramount importance. After a reasonable probationary period, you will be assessing each new employee's performance. If at that time an employee is failing to meet minimum requirements, you have three choices:

1. Extend the probationary period and provide additional training, coaching, and counseling.
2. Try to match the employee's skills and abilities by placing him or her in a different job.
3. Fire the employee.

You should seriously consider all three options, not shying away from the third one. You don't want to keep employees you don't respect. It isn't good for the business unit. If a probationary employee has enduring performance problems, the best solution may indeed be firing. After all, while you have made a mistake in hiring, the employee has made a comparable mistake in accepting the position, and is continuing to make mistakes on the job.

Test Validation

This chapter has repeatedly made the point that selection tools should be chosen on the basis of their demonstrated ability to predict performance. This is not merely a good idea; it is mandated by various EEO laws. But don't panic. You don't necessarily have to go outside the company to buy tests with impeccable pedigrees. Tests can be developed and validated in-house if you have people with the expertise to do it.

Here's how it's done. Begin with a basic question: "If I had been using this selection tool, how correct would my hiring decisions have been?" An example will show how to proceed. The CEO of a manufacturing firm asks his vice president of personnel to design a work-sample test to be used in selecting the new machine-tenders that the company hires each year. After doing her homework, the VP has the test administered to all candidates for that job during the year. But the scores on the test are *not* used in the selection process, since they are not yet validated. Instead they are put in a file drawer.

Six months or so later, when the first formal assessments are made of the new employees, the scores for the new machine-tenders are taken out of the file drawer and matched against the employees' actual performance. If the strength of the relationship between test scores and job performance is significant, both statistically and practically, the test can safely and effectively be used. It has been demonstrated that scores on the test accurately predict performance. But be careful: This kind of test development and validation cannot be handled by amateurs. Most managers do not have the training to do it, and consequently it is often better to assign the task to outside experts.

There is a common belief that compliance with EEO regulations leads to poor business decisions and prevents adequate assessment of job applicants. That really isn't true. Good business decisions and EEO compliance, as the example tends to demonstrate, go hand in hand. Test validation helps ensure that the tests used in the selection process are in fact predictive of job performance. There is nothing wrong with that. It will do you, the manager, at least as much good as it does the EEO watchdogs who are trying to eliminate unfair discrimination against women, blacks, and other groups that historically have been excluded from the economic mainstream.

Without worrying too much about legal complexities, you can assume that *any* information can be used in the selection process so long as:

1. The information has been demonstrated to predict job performance accurately and reliably.

2. Its use does not have an adverse effect on any sexual, racial, ethnic, religious, or age group.

Note, however, that having a valid test and actually using it do not always go hand in hand. The costs of using the test may be greater than the benefits it generates. Various selection utility models have been developed to determine the bottom-line impact on selection tests. These models are complicated but are often worth consulting to find out whether a specific test is worth developing and administering.

"You're Hired"

The task of hiring employees you can respect is anything but easy, but it is critical to your success as a manager. The work of your business unit is shared among all employees. If those employees are capable and effective, they will make you look good. If they are incompetent and lackadaisical, they will make you look bad. And it all began for each of those employees on the day you said, "You're hired."

Ten Points to Remember

1. In the hiring process, full disclosure by the manager will give the applicant a realistic picture of the job and the level of performance expected.
2. Job analysis can help match a prospective employee's skills and abilities with those demanded by the job.
3. The three best ways to generate a pool of job applicants are (a) referrals from present employees, (b) referrals from former employees; and (c) walk-ins.
4. Employment interviews are important for collecting and sharing information but have drawbacks as a selection tool.
5. An alternative to the interview is a Biographical Information Blank (BIB), a questionnaire concerning the applicant's past successes and failures.
6. A good aptitude test or tests can be helpful in predicting a candidate's potential for a particular kind of job.

7. Achievement and work-sample tests are especially useful; they ask a candidate to do basically what the job requires.

8. Hiring from within is an excellent practice if the goal is not to acquire a change agent.

9. Where future promotions are slated, the prospective employee should be qualified for each job called for in the plan.

10. Tests for employee selection must be validated to meet EEO requirements; this can sometimes be done in-house.

9

Effective Training

Y OU probably don't have to be convinced of the importance of
training. American organizations spend a lot of money each
year on training their employees. One conservative estimate from
the early 1980s puts the figure at $125 billion.

Although plenty of money is spent on training, much of it is
squandered. Instruction in the latest fad is commonplace, and nearly
all such training is a waste of time and money. To be worthwhile,
training must focus on the specific needs of the business unit. And
it must be presented in such a way as to produce the intended
outcome.

Essentials of Performance Training

The main focus of earlier chapters was the performance of stated job
requirements. This chapter is concerned with developmental activities to help employees meet or exceed the stated requirements of
their jobs. Let's call these activities *performance training*. As you will
see, performance training has been touched on in nearly every previous chapter. In this chapter the activities will be presented as five
basic learning objectives of a comprehensive program:

1. To understand fully the stated performance requirements of the
   assigned job
2. To recognize how meeting the stated performance requirements
   contributes to the business unit
3. To master the various demands of the job, closing the gap between the skills and abilities needed and those already possessed

4. To know when and how formal appraisals will show the degree to which performance requirements have been met

5. To understand what the organizational rewards are and how they will be allocated

Objective 1: To Understand Fully the Stated Performance Requirements of the Assigned Job

During the hiring process, you explained these requirements carefully. But a one-time explanation, particularly under the pressure of a job interview, is not sufficient to fix them firmly in the employee's mind. Your training program should reaffirm the performance requirements and clarify them so that no ambiguities exist. Employees must know exactly what is expected of them. Any doubts about these expectations should be resolved. Any questions about them should be answered. Employees cannot meet expectations of which they are unaware.

Objective 2: To Recognize How Meeting the Stated Performance Requirements Contributes to the Business Unit

Employees should know why they are expected to meet the particular requirements of their job. This understanding can have an indirect effect on performance, increasing job knowledge and enhancing motivation. Most people work more efficiently when they understand the reasons behind what they are doing. Knowing how the requirements were formulated increases the likelihood that expectations will be met. More than that, it gives employees a sense that the requirements are meaningful, that they contribute to the functioning of the entire business unit. Employees naturally want to feel that what they do on the job has an impact beyond the limited observable results.

Objective 3: To Master the Various Demands of the Job, Closing the Gap between the Skills and Abilities Needed and Those Already Possessed

This is the conventional core of a performance training program. The goal is to enable the employee to perform better on the job. In a formal sense, the skills and abilities demanded by the job are identified through the job analysis procedure described in the previous chapter. Those skills and abilities actually possessed by the employee are determined through testing procedures, also described in chapter 8. In many cases, the analyses will be less formal, however, since both the abilities and the deficiencies are often self-evident. And whatever the training needs are, the content of that training will obviously vary according to the particular job and employee.

It should be mentioned that the how-to training under this third objective can be broader than just the nuts-and-bolts instruction needed for an employee to meet minimum requirements. It can provide whatever other information will enable the employee to do his or her job—and to do it more capably. The training may involve aspects of product knowledge and process knowledge that bear directly on the employee's daily work. As a manager, you want to see more than barely satisfactory performance, and any training that will encourage better work is worth considering.

Objective 4: To Know When and How Formal Appraisals Will Show the Degree to Which Performance Requirements Have Been Met

Employees should receive full information on how and when formal performance appraisals will be made and feedback will occur. You should be sure that employees understand the purpose of the formal appraisal system. They will benefit, too, by knowing how the tools for appraisal were developed, how management uses them, and how the best performers will profit from the program.

Objective 5: To Understand What the Organizational Rewards Are and How They Will Be Allocated

As you know, money or any other motivational reward motivates performance only if employees see and believe that management pays for performance. Explain fully the reward system of your business unit. Don't leave out fringe benefits such as medical and dental insurance. In many companies, they are worth thousands of dollars a year to each employee. If certain kinds of rewards—stock in the company, for example—require definition or elaboration, take the time to provide this information. Your goal is to present the entire array of inducements your business unit offers employees and to show how each of the inducements can be earned.

Truth in Training

The foregoing learning objectives, if achieved, will help employees meet or exceed the stated performance requirements of their jobs. But a warning note should be sounded. Much of what is described here is idealized to some extent. It has to be in order to make the main points clear. And this creates no problem if the material presented to employees in their training sessions is honest—if it is based on what is actually happening and not on what you or the personnel department wishes were happening, and if it doesn't diverge too widely from the everyday reality your employees observe on the job.

Employees will be uneasy and even resentful if they keep thinking to themselves, "But that's not the way it is! That's not the way things happen here!" Keep in mind that you (or the people in personnel) may view the work situation very differently from the way employees view it. From your perspective, you may see a strategic plan in place and working well. You may think the reward system is eminently fair and ticking along like a Patek Phillippe.

From Jose Delgado's viewpoint, however (he's a young, hardworking clerk in finance), the most noteworthy circumstance is not the cosmic beauty of the strategic plan or its profitable execution. What he notices, or strongly suspects, is that the manager of his department is sleeping with Fifi LaFluff, a recently promoted, highly paid, moderately competent assistant who looks a bit like Bo Derek.

To pretend, in training or out, that such circumstances don't occur, or that they have no relevance to the smooth functioning of the system, is to be naive and to risk losing credibility. Jose is a realist. He knows damn well he isn't going to match Fifi's dazzling rise simply by working hard and exceeding his performance requirements.

This is not to suggest that a training program should become a forum for gossip. It shouldn't. On the other hand, neither you, nor personnel, nor anyone else involved in training should imply that a business-unit utopia is at hand. Your employees won't buy it. They know, and so do you, that no system comprised of human beings will ever be wholly without flaws or inequities.

Beyond the Call of Duty

Now to look on the bright side: Just as you may have a few bad apples despite all your safeguards, so will you have some very good apples. These are the employees who make spontaneous and innovative contributions to the business unit, people who are committed, able, and sufficiently respected to exceed what you have told them is required. They add creativity and inventiveness to the business unit. They often do the unexpected, going well beyond the call of duty. These are the employees who truly make a business unit thrive.

To encourage people to become such "good citizens" of an organization requires a different kind of developmental effort from performance training. However, performance training is a prerequisite. An employee isn't likely to make the kind of good-citizen contributions you want unless he or she has mastered the job and is fully meeting its requirements.

The training activities that can help employees become good citizens will be referred to as *business civics education*. Think back to your high school civics course. Perhaps it was called political science, or government, or citizenship education. Whatever its name, the purpose of the course was to help you understand how the executive, legislative, and judicial branches of government work and to see how they relate to one another through a system of checks and balances. Such an understanding is important to you in performing your role as a citizen in the community, state, and nation.

In much the same way, business civics education is designed to help employees understand the role of their business unit in the industry and, more broadly, in the economic, political, and social environment. Such an understanding is important if employees are to perform effectively as citizens in the business unit.

Here are the two learning objectives of a comprehensive program:

1. To understand the relationship between the business unit and its competitors
2. To appreciate the nature of the relationship between the overall environment and the industry of which the business unit is a part

These may seem to be remarkably broad objectives for new employees. They are worth pursuing, though, if you want to create the best work force possible. Let's look at each one.

Objective 1: To Understand the Relationship between the Business Unit and Its Competitors

Competition is at the heart of American business. Employees know this, but many of them see it in vague or even theoretical terms. Your goal is to bring it home to them. To do so, you will compare and contrast:

The *products* of the business unit with those of its major competitors, focusing on essential product characteristics. This isn't a sales pitch. You want your employees to appreciate, if not admire, the tough competition that is out there.

The *performance* of the business unit with that of its major competitors, focusing on profits, ROI, and measures of labor efficiency. Again, this shouldn't be puffery. By the same token, if the comparison isn't favorable, you don't want to make it sound like a veiled accusation.

When employees complete a program of this sort, they should have a greater knowledge of the competitive market system in which their business unit operates. They should be especially aware of the unit's competitive advantages and disadvantages. Most of all, they should see that business decisions are not made in a vacuum. They should understand that competitive forces drive much of the activity of the business.

Objective 2: To Appreciate the Nature of the Relationship between the Overall Environment and the Industry of Which the Business Unit is a Part

This objective, although broad, is clear-cut. The size and scope of your business will determine to a great extent the nature of the training. In a unit of a large corporation, you might want to go into how international monetary exchange rates affect industry exports. Or you might want to explain how federal safety laws affect characteristics of the industry's products.

In a relatively small or local business, your approach would be different. You might want to explain the general business history and present the economic makeup of the community. Or you might want to describe how state and local regulations affect your day-to-day activities.

Even at the local level, these are complex matters, and business civics education is not intended to produce an expert level of knowledge. It is basically an informative overview designed to heighten sensitivity. As such, it should be presented to *all* employees, not just those in the higher echelons. All employees can benefit from it, although certainly the education and experience of employees have to be considered. If employees know the language of business and economics, the instruction can proceed at a rapid pace. If they don't, then time must be taken to define terms and clarify concepts. A CPA with an MBA won't need an explanation of ROI. A machine-tender with a high school education probably will.

As common sense suggests, performance training should precede business civics education. Performance training should begin for a new employee as soon as possible after hiring. But bear in mind that neither kind of instruction is a one-time event. As employees change jobs within the business unit, or as the performance requirements of current jobs change, additional performance training will be necessary. If fairly dramatic shifts occur in the relationship between the business unit and its overall environment, employees should be informed through business civics education.

Seven learning objectives have been specified—five for performance training, two for business civics education. Your training dollars should be concentrated on these seven areas. Any training program not designed with at least one of them in mind is probably a waste of time. Don't spend money on the latest fad. Manage smart.

Training the Smart Manager

The seven objectives apply to managers as well as to other employees. Managers need both performance training and business civics education. The content of the instruction will be different, of course, with much heavier emphasis on how to deal with people. To be a successful manager, you must be able to apply the three Rs. To do so with confidence and authority, you have to understand and work with people. That may sound easy, but it isn't. The skills and abilities necessary for managing people are broad, diverse, and demanding. Very few inexperienced managers can handle people well. They simply don't know how yet. They need time to learn, to develop, to mature. Training can be invaluable, assuming that the trainee has managerial potential.

Ideally, the in-house people who are likely to be promoted to managerial positions should be identified and developed for those jobs prior to promotion. This gives them a chance to be "groomed"—the old-school synonym for "trained." Prospective managers can be instructed in how to conduct appraisal feedback sessions (to take a single example) with highly positive results. Indeed, the right kind of training for prospective managers can produce tremendous payoffs.

Yet more dollars are probably wasted on developing managers than on any other training effort. Those glossily promoted "how to be an effective manager" training seminars are as common as the sere leaves in autumn and just about as moldy. A few are okay, to be sure, but most are useless, which is a shame, because no one denies that the corporate world is in need of authentic leaders. Later chapters will address this age-old and always fascinating subject of leadership.

Ten Points to Remember

1. Employee training should focus on the specific needs of the business unit, not on current fads.

2. A good training program explores performance requirements in depth, clarifying them so that no ambiguities exist.

3. Employees who understand why particular requirements were formulated are more likely to meet these requirements.

4. The core of performance training involves helping the employee gain those skills and abilities needed to meet or exceed minimum requirements.

5. The formal performance appraisal system should be fully explained.

6. Employees need to be told of the entire reward system, including fringe benefits, and to learn how various rewards can be earned.

7. Training must be honest and perceptive; no one should suggest that every aspect of the system works perfectly.

8. One way to encourage employees to be good citizens of the business unit is to give them an understanding of the competitive market in which the business operates.

9. Employees can also benefit from an overview of their industry's place in the economic, political, and social environment.

10. Managers require training somewhat similar to that of other employees, but with heavier emphasis on dealing with people.

10

Techniques of Performance Training

T HE content of training is of the utmost importance, as the last chapter noted. So is the presentation of that content. The subject matter can be entirely appropriate, the goal worthy, the potential results well worth the time and money expended, but if content is delivered in an inappropriate way, the training will fail. It will not produce the intended results. Your time and money will have been wasted.

How do you decide what training technique to use? You look at the obvious elements:

The *content* to be delivered

The *employees* at whom it is aimed

The *cost*

Simple, but still vague. The truth is that no one knows how to weigh and combine those three elements to yield optimum results. According to Dr. Ken Wexley of Michigan State University and Dr. Gary Latham of the University of Washington, in their book *Developing and Training Human Resources in Organizations*, your best guide is common sense. Gee, thanks a lot, you say. Still, there's no better guide in the short run than your intuitive analysis of what training techniques ought to work.

In the long run, of course, you can evaluate the effectiveness of your choices. Over time, you will get an increasingly clear picture of what succeeds for you in your business unit. This picture will lead to more effective choices in the future. Let's explore the various options.

On-the-Job Training

At your local bank, you've probably fidgeted while a newly hired teller moved uncertainly though the steps of a routine procedure under the watchful eyes of an experienced teller. This hands-on process slows down operations for the moment, but it prevents costly errors, and it gives the new teller specific, direct, valuable experience.

The intent of on-the-job training is to develop skills and abilities necessary for an employee to meet stated performance requirements of the job. Each trainee is observed by an experienced employee who offers immediate instruction and feedback. If the trainer, the experienced employee, is well chosen and prepared, on-the-job instruction can be highly effective—and cost-effective.

One point to remember: Trainers must be told explicitly what is required, and they must be reviewed and rewarded accordingly. You don't want that experienced bank teller, for instance, frustrated at the increasing length of the line in the bank, to elbow the trainee unceremoniously out of the way and put on a burst of speed and efficiency while the trainee stands by bewildered and resentful.

Special cases of on-the-job training include understudy assignments, internships, and apprenticeships. An understudy is typically being trained for a senior management position. An intern is gaining supervised practical experience. An apprentice is ordinarily learning a skilled trade.

Coaching and Counseling

Coaching and counseling were mentioned in connection with formal performance appraisal. The techniques are particularly useful with:

New employees

Employees with performance problems

Employees being groomed for promotion

As with on-the-job training, coaching and counseling must become a stated and evaluated part of the manager's job if it is to work.

Only a small number of managers are self-starting coaches and counselors. They don't usually regard employee training as a path to advancement. Therefore, incentives have to be built in.

Job Rotation: Pluses and Minuses

The theory is fine. An employee spends a relatively brief time on one job, then another, then another. By moving in this way, the employee supposedly get a a broad perspective of the business unit and sees firsthand how the individual parts interact. Supposedly. It frequently fails.

Job rotation seems like such an obviously good idea to some managers that they neglect to specify the learning objectives attached to the moves. The moves appear good in and of themselves. But are they? It's often not clear what the employee who moves from one job to another is actually gaining. Most employees to whom the senior author has talked see job rotation as primarily serving a warehousing function. The employees regard themselves as being held in temporary storage, waiting to get a "real" job assignment.

There is, however, another side to this coin. If job rotation is carefully planned, if the learning objectives are well designed, and if appraisals are made along the way—in short, if job rotation is structured and not amorphous—it can work. The problem is that this ideal state is so hard to achieve (or else is viewed as pointless by trainers, trainees, or both) that job rotation cannot be recommended as a technique likely to be effective.

Lectures and Their Offshoots

Many trainers, like college instructors and high school teachers, enjoy lecturing. But be wary. The lecture method has limitations. Lectures are unlikely to help employees to develop their skills and abilities. They just aren't very functional when it comes to learning how to *do* something. Imagine trying to teach a person to type by using the lecture technique. You wouldn't get far. Neither would the typist.

On the other hand, lectures can be fine for teaching *about* something. The distinction is important. A student typist would get little or nothing out of a lecture, but a management trainee could learn a good deal about the history of the company through the lecture

method. Lectures don't teach behaviors, but they can convey descriptive information. Thus, lectures have to be coupled with other
techniques in the how-to area, but can stand alone in the this-is-how-
it-is area.

Lectures can be deadly, of course. Every college graduate has
probably had at least one instructor who was better than a pill at
putting students to sleep. For training managers, it's a good idea to
combine straight lectures with such techniques as case studies, role
playing, and games.

Case Studies

A case study presents trainees with a written description of a business problem. After trainees read the problem, they identify its fac-
ets and devise workable solutions. It sounds like a can't-miss technique for enhancing a trainee's ability to solve business problems
analytically. Unfortunately, it isn't. Most of the cases used in management development are too general. They don't address the problems that managers actually face on the job. They are all right for
business schools, where the training is necessarily general, but for a
specific job the cases need to be job specific. If they are, good. If
they aren't, you should probably use something else.

Role Playing

In role playing, trainees act out their responses to a problem. If trainees' performances are directly relevant to the job, role playing can
be an excellent technique. A police-detective trainee interrogating a
role-playing suspect is an example of a situation where role playing
is the obvious approach. A sales representative trying to overcome
objections or close a sale is also a ready-made situation for role
playing.

Games

As a rule, games involve having trainees participate in running a
simulated business unit. Games can be fun and, consequently, are
quite popular. But fun is not the object of training. You will want to
look at off-the-shelf management games with a skeptical eye. What
are their learning objectives? How relevant are they to your business

unit? A hard look is likely to result in no purchase. Tailor-made games are another matter, though. These games simulate your own business unit and usually have clear-cut objectives. They can be highly useful, but, being customized, they are often expensive to develop and maintain.

Audiovisual Techniques

In American education, AV was touted decades ago as the wave of the future. The wave never really broke on the schoolroom curriculum (it may still be coming), but it has definitely washed over business in general and business training in particular. The AV storeroom can hold a lot of related media—movies, slides, filmstrips, records, audio cassettes, video cassettes, and more. Audiovisual materials have frequently been used to supplement lectures, but technology has been making stand-alone AV training packages readily available.

These AV packages have their advantages. Many things can be put on a videotape cassette (today's main medium of choice) that cannot be demonstrated in any practical way by a lecturer. Then, too, if large numbers of employees are to be trained in several geographic locations, stand-alone AV techniques are likely to be cheaper than a traveling lecturer or an itinerant dog-and-pony show. Of course, you can't talk back to a piece of AV equipment. Not yet, but who knows what the future holds?

The subject of AV devices as training tools is a vast and fascinating one, well covered in specialized books. One final note is in order. Making or buying appropriate audio cassettes for sales reps and others who spend a great deal of time in company cars is a step worth considering. Instead of listening to Waylon Jennings, your man in Kentucky can tune in at his convenience to your director of marketing (or to Lee Iacocca). Instead of listening to "Ask Dr. Brothers," your woman in Delaware can learn about the sales features of a new product and the strategies for selling it.

Using Programmed Instruction

Programmed instruction has managed to acquire an undeservedly bad name over the past twenty years. The reason is that the technique was promoted and sold before a workable technology for it existed. The basic idea behind programmed instruction is sound and appealing. The idea is self-teaching. In programmed instruction, a trainee achieves specified learning objectives while working at his or her own pace. The learning sequence is logical and highly structured, a sequence that demands continuing self-evaluation and, if necessary, remedial action.

The concept is fine, but the early programs were pitiful. Some of them were programmed textbooks. Some were so-called teaching machines. At their best, these materials promoted rapid learning. At their worst, they turned bored-out-of-their-gourd trainees (or public-school students) into rebels at the barricades. In a corporate setting, to add to the difficulties, the development of useful programmed materials was, and is, expensive.

Despite all this, programmed instruction has a respectable present and a possibly brilliant future. That's because the needed technology is now in place. The powerful instrument of programmed instruction is the personal computer (PC), which has become a teaching machine, and a spectacularly good one. Various software programs of *computer-assisted instruction* (CAI) or *computer-based training* (CBT)—two names for the same thing—are appearing with increasing frequency. Some are excellent.

Programmed instruction, once almost dead, is rising like a phoenix. The ready availability, along with the proven appeal, of personal computers is likely to increase reliance on programmed instruction as a training method. PC training may or may not be a cost-effective means of instruction, but there is no question that computers have a magnetic attraction for managers and employees alike. The forward-looking manager will pay close attention to the latest developments in computer training software.

The Power of Behavior Modeling

Behavior modeling is just what the name implies. It involves observing the behaviors of others and noting the consequences of those behaviors. Babies use behavior modeling all the time. So do adults. When you see a person touch a stove, howl in pain, and jump back, you conclude that the stove is hot. You don't touch it.

Employees often model the behavior of their managers. Behavior modeling is a prevalent and frequently unconscious way of learning.

People will use the technique whether management recommends it or not. It's hard *not* to use.

During the 1970s, behavior modeling began to be incorporated in a formal way into many business training programs. When thus taught, it includes the following:

Introduction of the behaviors to be learned (what they are and why they are important)

Exposure of trainees to the model (trainees observe someone engaging in the behaviors in the desired way)

Explanation of what, precisely, constitutes the desired way

Practice of the desired behaviors by the trainees in the desired way

Feedback to the trainees on their performance

It may sound a little stodgy, but in practice it isn't. Behavior modeling often incorporates other ways of training, such as lectures, audiovisual materials, and role playing. The technique has much to recommend it, not the least of which is that trainees observe in practice exactly what they are supposed to do. There is no intermediate agent of instruction—the trainer is actually doing what he or she is teaching.

Group Processes—Maybe

There are legions of managers who love this technique. It's a lot of fun to jet off to Marriott's Camelback Inn, or Cloister Sea Island, or the Greenbrier, there to share various high-level aspects of corporate lore. The supposed benefits (the ones related to managerial development) are fairly obvious. You get away from those constant office interruptions. You get to know your peers better, which perhaps helps all of you to work more effectively together. You get to know yourself better, to understand your strengths and weaknesses as a manager.

Do those goals sound a bit fuzzy? They are. In fact, ambiguity regarding intended consequences is a common feature of these five-star corporate retreats. What are the learning objectives out there on the shores of Lake Tahoe? How is the group meeting designed to achieve those objectives? The senior author has examined a number of such group-process affairs and has rarely found outcomes to justify the expenditure of training dollars. Maybe other good purposes are served, but training?—seldom.

Let's Not Forget Reading

"Oh-oh," you're thinking, "here we go from boffo Bimini to boring books."

Well, yes, but reading is a proven method of learning, one that can be used to a far greater degree than it has been so far in business. Reading, even if costly technical books have to be purchased, is relatively cheap. (How much per day does a room at the Broadmoor cost?) Reading is convenient. (The book comes to the trainee; the trainee doesn't have to catch a flight to the book.) Reading can be personalized. (Instead of a vague rap session, the trainee can get specific answers on specific subjects.)

Reading is not the be-all and end-all, of course, and any reading assignment should be coupled with some mechanism for making sure the trainee actually does the reading. No one will willingly skip a stay at the Doral Hotel and Country Club, but plenty of managers will avoid reading a book if there's a convenient way out. Even so, you should think seriously about using reading as a training tool. It's a good one.

The Choice Is Yours

Nine training techniques have been mentioned. More exist, and more are probably on the way. You have plenty of options. If your business unit has a data base to guide your decision making, by all means use it. If not, use your judgment. Base your choice on what appears to be the best technique, or mix of techniques, for achieving the *known* objectives.

Don't put the cart before the horse. Don't choose a technique first and then ask what objective it can serve. If you do, it's rather like the Red Queen in *Alice in Wonderland*: "Sentence first," screams the Queen at Alice's trial, "verdict afterwards." It's foolish, but it does happen.

In making your choice, take sales pitches for what they are. Training packages are marketed aggressively. Buy only when you have judged a package to be satisfactory for meeting *your* needs. Don't let a marketer tell you what your needs are.

Smart Managers Evaluate

Naturally, you want to build on success. At the opposite extreme, you don't want to follow lemmings over a cliff. Since the results of training are so important—and not always perfectly clear—you need ways of evaluating whether your training efforts have achieved their objectives.

The previous chapter dealt with seven learning objectives, five in performance training, two in business civics education. Any training effort should be designed to meet one or more of those objectives. The objectives were stated in general terms. In practice, you will have to state them in specific terms. For example, the first of the general objectives was this: "To understand fully the stated performance requirements of the assigned job." There's nothing wrong with that except its cosmic scope. For a group of middle managers, that requirement might become, "To learn how to give more effective performance feedback to one's employees."

In this case, training should produce an improvement in behavior. That is what needs to be evaluated. Don't ask trainees whether they like or dislike the training program. That doesn't measure anything. It doesn't tell you if learning objectives were attained. You need measurement, not guff.

Here's an illustration of the right way to measure a training program. Take the performance-feedback objective above. Suppose that eighty managers are to go through a training program aimed at achieving that objective. (To refresh your memory, you may want to look back at the specifics of performance feedback in chapter 5.) Although you intend to train eighty managers, your first step is to choose forty managers randomly. These forty managers complete the training program. Sometime later—before the second forty take the course—you ask the employees of all eighty managers to complete a questionnaire. This questionnaire contains items like, "Was your last performance appraisal session with your manager conducted without interruptions?" The idea is to measure the feedback behaviors of all eighty managers.

The responses of employees whose managers completed the training program are then statistically compared to those of employees whose managers have not yet taken the course. If the employees of the trained managers report significantly better performance-feedback behaviors, the training program has achieved its objective. If there is no significant difference, it hasn't, and the program needs to be redesigned.

It's an Ongoing Process

There are three points about training that still need to be made. Although the three have been alluded to earlier, they have not yet been pinned down. The three are transferability, reinforcement, and lifelong learning.

Transferability

When training takes place anywhere except on the job, the question of transferability arises. Can the new behavior, learned in a classroom setting, be successfully carried over to the job? If it can't, the utility of the training program is nil. The best way to help ensure transferability is to make the training situation and the job situation as nearly alike as possible. It's also worthwhile to use specific examples that show trainees how training-program content applies directly to the job.

Reinforcement

Training is often used in implementing organizational change. When it is, new behaviors are being introduced into the business unit. Unless the newly learned behaviors are reinforced on the job, they will not be retained. Enter the three Rs. Make the new behaviors:

- Requirements of the job, then
- Review and
- Reward them accordingly.

Lifelong Learning

The world, having been through Future Shock and Megatrends, knows by now that what a student learns in college may be obsolete within a couple of years on the job. Moreover, job requirements change, and employees change jobs. In both cases, additional training becomes necessary. You should tell new employees at the outset that their business life will be a continuing learning experience. In telling them, you may discover that some employees who hated school look forward eagerly to the challenge of business training.

Ten Points to Remember

1. On-the-job training, where possible, is especially effective because it gives the trainee direct work experience along with specific guidance.

2. Coaching and counseling are good for new employees, those with performance problems, and those slated for promotion.

3. Job rotation, when carefully structured and evaluated, may achieve its goals, but its track record is not impressive.

4. Lectures should be combined with case studies, role playing, games, and other teaching methods for maximum effectiveness.

5. Audiovisual media—videotape cassettes in particular—have become increasingly important and useful in business training.

6. Programmed instruction has outgrown its early failures; computer software has many applications and a bright future.

7. Formal behavior modeling is a sophisticated training technique that shows rather than tells the employee what to do.

8. Group interaction in a faraway resort has plenty of glamor but, as a training method, is seldom worth the expense.

9. Reading is a proven method of learning, one that is cheap, convenient, and subject-matter specific.

10. If you are to build on success, training programs must be evaluated for effectiveness; they may need to be adjusted or redesigned to make them as valid as possible.

11

Participatory Management

I 'M a great believer in participatory management," said Terry
Shields. "It makes good business sense."

"Do you use it yourself, then?"

"Well, no. I don't think we're quite ready for it at Backwater Beverages. It takes a certain kind of company, doesn't it? A microchip
outfit or something like that. I'm probably old-fashioned. I figure it's
my job to make the decisions here at Backwater. Participatory management is a good idea . . . in theory, I mean . . . but—"

Terry Shields is not alone. Many managers talk as if participatory
management is the way to go, but only a few of them go that way.
They can intellectually identify with more democratic ways of managing people. They know that participatory management has gotten
a good press. But when the chips are on the table, they play the
same cautious old game they have always played.

Although Terry would never admit it, he doesn't respect his employees. Why? Probably because the three Rs aren't being practiced
at Backwater Beverages. If they were, Terry could comfortably
move beyond the basics and apply the fourth R, respect. By doing
so, he could take full advantage of the contributions his employees
could make but, under the Shields autocracy, won't.

Some managers think that participatory management is the polar
opposite of top-down management. It isn't. A participatory approach can succeed only if management accepts its traditional responsibilities. Management is and should be vested with consider-
able power, which it must exercise in appropriate ways. In a
participatory approach, management *selectively* shares some of the
power with employees. What is shared . . . and when . . . and how
. . . and with whom—all these remain the province of management.

What Are the Benefits?

Okay, you say. I'll try to apply—selectively—a participatory approach. What benefits can I expect?

First, here's the wet blanket: You should *not* expect a participatory approach to have a direct, short-term effect on how well your employees perform their stated job requirements.

Wait a minute. That doesn't sound right. Nonetheless, it is. The results of many rigorously conducted studies clearly indicate that while participation has a favorable impact on employees' job satisfaction, it doesn't influence performance. Or, more accurately, it doesn't influence performance on routinely assigned day-to-day tasks. Perhaps that explains in part why employee participation programs have never taken the business world by storm. They have been around since the turn of the century, and in most business units they come and go. They have not been so consistently successful that hordes of managers are clamoring to get on board.

The general failure of employee participation programs has two root causes: (1) poor implementation; (2) unrealistic management expectations. In other words, the idea isn't flawed, but the perception and the execution of it often are.

Long-term Effects

Time is the stream that successful participatory management has to go a-fishing in. As stated earlier, a participatory approach has no direct, short-term effect on how well your employees perform their stated job requirements. That is far from saying it has no effects at all. The effects it has are long-term.

There is clear evidence that, over time, a participatory approach can enhance employee satisfaction, which in turn can pay off in positive ways. Participation can lead to increased attachment to the business unit, reducing levels of absenteeism and turnover and thereby reducing labor costs and having a favorable impact on productivity. It can also enhance psychological commitment to the business unit, encouraging employees to become what were earlier termed good citizens.

Good citizens go beyond merely meeting stated performance requirements. They contribute altruism, extra effort, and new ideas to the business unit. As a rule, their acts of good citizenship are not headline-grabbing, but are more subtle. Dr. Daniel Katz of the University of Michigan identifies a few:

A production worker notices and tells a nearby co-worker that her machine is getting jammed.

A typist comes to the aid of a co-worker who is behind in meeting her performance requirements for the day.

A group of salespersons on their own suggest a new advertising campaign as a means of attracting an undertapped market segment.

Two computer operators develop a new procedure for assigning priorities to jobs, thereby reducing waiting time.

These are good-citizenship activities. Although they cannot be explicitly programmed, a participatory approach, working properly, can encourage them. It can also sustain them by providing a formal means (a suggestion box is the familiar example) for translating good-citizenship activities into solid, continuing contributions.

Before adopting a participatory approach, you must be well satisfied with the present condition of the business unit. The three Rs should be in place and functioning. Participatory management will succeed only in a stable business environment.

When a company is in chaos, this dash of democracy will simply create more chaos—and probably cost a great deal of money as the system comes unglued.

With that said, it's time to look at how to begin with participatory management.

How to Begin

As you set off down the road to participatory management, you come immediately to a Y intersection. The arrow to the left reads "Employee Initiative." The arrow to the right says "Seeking Involvement."

The road to the left, "Employee Initiative," depends on employees coming forward on their own to make suggestions and become involved in activities that go beyond their stated performance requirements. You, the manager, must provide structure to encourage these self-initiatives. When employees act on their own, you should (if you are aware of the actions) respond appropriately. The less structured of the two kinds of participatory management, this approach is not the main focus of this chapter.

The road to the right, "Seeking Involvement," demands that you actively request employee involvement. It gives you much greater responsibility, and it requires you to choose the specifics of the involvement—when, how, who. This kind of participatory approach is the more challenging one and has greater potential than the self-initiative plan.

Whichever approach you choose, though, remember that you are the boss. You have to make the decisions. No matter which fork of the road you travel, you are responsible for managing the involvement of your employees. You cannot place that responsibility and authority in the hands of your employees. To do so would produce not democracy but anarchy.

Seeking Employee Involvement

"You are cordially invited. . . ."

When you seek out involvement from your employees, you are inviting them to participate in making a decision. You have told them, in effect, that you have chosen not to make a certain decision unilaterally, but instead want to include others in the decision-making process.

Two big advantages stem from this choice. According to the late University of Michigan psychologist N.R.F. Maier, you can expect:

Improved *quality* of decisions

Increased *ease* of implementing decisions

It's easy to see why these results can be achieved. The participants you choose are ones with relevant knowledge, information, or experience. The sum of their knowledge is greater than that available to you acting alone. Moreover, the varying experience brought to bear on the issue can give you a broader perspective. Implementation is easier because employees who participate in making a decision understand it better and are more likely to accept it. A unilateral decision by management has to be sold to employees. A participative decision doesn't. If some of the employees are chosen primarily to help in implementation (rather than to provide expertise for the decision itself), the task should be easier still. At its best, participatory decision making can greatly reduce misunderstandings and resistance as the decision is implemented and change occurs.

Conditions to Be Met

Given the advantages to be gained from employee participation, why not involve them in all decisions you have to make? That question is addressed in *Managerial Process and Organizational Behavior*, a book by Dr. Alan Filley of the University of Wisconsin and Dr. Robert House of the University of Toronto. They list a number of conditions that must be met if employees are to contribute meaningfully to making a decision:

The decision is not routine. Mundane operational decisions are made day in and day out. To invoke participatory management for all of them would bring business to a halt. This is not to say that participatory management cannot be used to improve routine matters, but only to suggest that the method is generally more appropriate to nonroutine ones.

The information for making the decision is not standard or centralized. This goes hand in hand with the nonroutine requirement. If a manual, or a computer data base, or an individual employee already has all the standardized information needed to make a decision, why bring together a group of less-informed employees?

The decision does not have to be made rapidly. Groups take longer than individuals to make decisions. Typically, they don't just take longer, they take *much* longer. If a decision has to be made quickly, you don't have the time to invite participation. It's as simple as that. The decision is yours; it has to be. Pressures of this kind are most common in a turbulent business environment. A turbulent environment is one characterized by a continuing series of unpredictable changes, any one or all of which can alter a unit's competitive position. Turbulence is usually evident in an entire industry. Thus, when participatory management won't work because of the time factor in company X, it probably won't work in company Y or Z within the same industry.

Employee participation is legitimate, and employees can make a genuine contribution. A kind of pseudoparticipatory management, in which employees are invited but irrelevant to the outcome, is a mistake. The participatory process should start only when you, as a manager, are committed to using the approach as a means for reaching a nonunilateral decision. Participatory management should not be used as a smokescreen to ease implementation of unpopular decisions from on high.

Whom *Not* to Involve

The owners of a chain of hot dog stands, Pup 'n' Kraut, decided to sell the chain to a holding company. They made the decision because they felt it was to their economic advantage. In making the decision, the owners did not consult with the three hundred or so part-time employees who staffed their street-corner hot dog stands. The Pup 'n' Kraut employees took it stoically, as you might expect. "It's their company," said one. "It ain't mine. I'll work just as hard for Foodwise Investments as I did for the Edelmans."

More complex are the situations in which technical expertise is the overriding consideration. In such cases, you are likely to turn to technical experts, even though they may not be the ones directly affected by the decision.

For example, the manager of a plant that makes consumer electronics has to decide whether or not to replace several machines used in the manufacturing process. The men and women who tend those machines will obviously be affected by the decision. However, the employees, although semiskilled, do not have the background to understand the engineering or financial aspects of the replacement decision. The manager therefore chooses not to involve the machine-tenders in the decision-making process. Instead, she seeks advice from electrical and industrial engineers and a financial analyst. She is right to handle it this way, because employee involvement would be neither meaningful nor helpful.

Five Decision-making Options

Some of what has been said is discussed in an important book, *Leadership and Decision Making*, by Dr. Victor Vroom of Yale University and his Australian colleague, Dr. Philip Yetton. They present five options for involving (or not involving) employees in making decisions.

1. The manager makes the decision autonomously, using information already available to him or her at the time.
2. The manager makes the decision autonomously, obtaining necessary information from employees on a one-to-one basis.
3. The manager makes the decision autonomously, obtaining not only information but also ideas and suggestions from employees on a one-to-one basis.
4. The manager makes the decision autonomously, obtaining information, ideas, and suggestions from some or all employees in a group meeting.
5. The manager, acting as chairperson of the group, makes the decision along with his or her employees.

Option 1 obviously represents a conventional top-down strategy, while option 5 shows the greatest adherence to a participatory management approach. Options 2 through 4 are progressively more consultative in nature. But notice that in four of the five options the manager is making the decision autonomously.

Seven Rules for Decision Makers

In their book, Vroom and Yetton go well beyond laying out the options. They also present rules to guide managers in making the right choices. Generally speaking, there is no one best choice in a given set of circumstances; several options may be acceptable. If so, you must rely on your own judgment and your own management style. Don't try to be something you're not.

Here are the rules:

Rule One

If the quality of a decision is important, and if you, the manager, lack sufficient information to make a good decision, choose a consultative option (2, 3, 4, or 5).

Quality has to do with whether a decision is objectively good or bad. Sometimes you can't determine quality. In those instances, quality is not important; it is simply not at issue.

Rule Two

If acceptance by employees is critical, and if they are unlikely to accept your unilateral decision, choose an option that seeks information, ideas, and suggestions from employees (3, 4, or 5).

Employee acceptance is critical if the decision cannot be implemented without it. In such cases, you must avoid a power play that renders the decision unacceptable.

Rule Three

If the quality of a decision is important, and if you have insufficient information to make a good decision, and if you don't know exactly what information is needed or where to get it, choose an option that encourages group interaction (4 or 5).

As noted earlier, groups can often produce higher-quality decisions than individuals. This is particularly true for the kind of unstructured problem described here. Group interaction can unlock the creative potential of the group members.

Rule Four

If acceptance by employees is critical, and if they are unlikely to accept your unilateral decision, and if *all* employees must be committed to the decision for it to work, choose an option that encourages group interaction (4 or 5).

Here you must reach a decision with which *all* employees can agree. Such a consensus, needed for the decision to be implemented, may well require some give-and-take among group members.

Rule Five

If the quality of a decision is important, and if you lack sufficient information to make a good decision, and if acceptance by employees is critical, and if they are unlikely to accept your unilateral decision, choose the straight participatory approach (5).

There are a lot of ifs here which, taken together, lead you to agree to adopt a decision by committee.

Rule Six

If acceptance by employees is critical, and if they are unlikely to accept your unilateral decision, and if a mutually beneficial decision is likely, choose the straight participatory approach (5).

Rule Six is much like Rule Four except that the commitment of each employee is not required here. With Rule Six, the hope is for a truly optimal decision, one that benefits you as well as all employees. To achieve that end, you give up decision-making autonomy. (In Rule Four, group interaction is required for obtaining agreement, but there is a good chance that a mutually beneficial decision will *not* result. Consequently, you might well decide to choose option 4, retaining autonomy.)

Rule Seven

If the quality of a decision is important, and if you lack sufficient information to make a good decision, and if employees have conflicting vested interests in alternative decisions, choose a consultative option, but avoid the straight participatory approach (2, 3, or 4).

You can easily see the need to referee among conflicting interests. When the showdown comes, you are the one who has to choose the winners and losers. It's a mistake to assume that right is always on the side of the big battalions.

Applying the Rules

These seven rules and the five options preceding them present an intricate mosaic of guidelines. Let's look at two examples of their application.

Nadine Berkowitz, marketing vice president for Avocado Computers, has to decide whether to add a unique, pocket-sized, Hong Kong–made computer to Avocado's line. By asking herself a series of questions, she determines that (a) quality is a factor; (b) she lacks sufficient information to make a good decision; (c) she doesn't know exactly what information is needed or where to get it; and (d) acceptance of the decision by employees is not critical. Taking those answers and applying the appropriate rule (Rule Five), Berkowitz finds that her choice is between one of the two group interaction options, 4 or 5. She chooses 4.

Dorsey Pickett, a school superintendent in South Carolina, faces a decision concerning a change in the district's program for gifted and talented students. He determines that (a) quality is a factor; (b) he has sufficient information to make a good decision; (c) acceptance by employees is critical; (d) they are unlikely to accept his unilateral decision; and (e) a mutually beneficial decision is likely. Taking those answers and applying the appropriate rule (Rule Six), Pickett chooses option 5, the straight participatory approach.

Remember that certain conditions must be met before applying the seven rules. They are critically important, and you may want to look back at pages 115–116 to refresh your memory.

Devising a personal strategy for seeking out involvement from your employees is no easy task. You will have to do some thinking, some experimenting, and probably some soul-searching. Be as honest with yourself as you can. Then make your choice and act. Over a fairly short period of time, you will probably find that your choices come easier, and your confidence in those choices is greatly enhanced.

The Employee-Initiative Path

You may recall the Y intersection early in this chapter. When you reached it, you took a right and followed the Seeking Involvement path. The next chapter will continue on that path, but a word needs to be said about the left-hand path, Employee Initiative.

This is a well-traveled path, and it can lead to excellent results when taken seriously. For it to succeed, you must communicate to your employees in ringing words that:

You wholeheartedly welcome their initiatives.

Their initiatives will be fairly and accurately evaluated.

Their initiatives will be rewarded, where appropriate.

An employee-initiative system does not have to be formalized, although that will sometimes help. The good old suggestion box has its virtues. If you use it, make sure your employees know how their suggestions will be evaluated and what kinds of rewards are in the business unit's cookie jar. Ideally, the rewards should be public recognition plus money.

Another approach, less frequently used, involves establishing a policy to encourage employees to recruit job applicants for the business unit. This policy should include rewards for successful recruiters—that is, employees who bring in applicants who are hired.

Regardless of the approach you use to encourage employee initiative, state your policy, and then restate it frequently. You must convince your employees that their potential contributions are wanted and needed. Assure them that any initiatives from them will get careful consideration and, when warranted, will receive worthwhile recognition.

Ten Points to Remember

1. Participatory management is an aspect of the smart manager's fourth R: respect.
2. The benefits of the participatory approach are long-term, good-citizen effects rather than direct, short-term ones.
3. Two types of participatory approaches exist: (a) the employee-initiative type; (b) the seeking-involvement type.
4. Inviting employees to participate in decision making can help improve the quality of decisions and make it easier to implement them.
5. A number of specific conditions must be met if employees are to contribute meaningfully to decision making.

6. Not all employees have sufficient background or technical expertise for involvement in management decisions.

7. Participatory options range from the top-down strategy (the manager as autocrat) to the straight participatory approach (the manager as chairperson).

8. In a participatory situation, the manager may deal with employees on a one-to-one basis, in a small group, or in a large group.

9. Specific guidelines exist for deciding how much employee participation to use under given circumstances.

10. If it is to succeed, the employee-initiative approach requires clear and repeated endorsements from management.

12

Developing a Participatory Approach

O NLY one of the five decision-making options has no employee participants. That's the first one, in which you, the manager, already have all the information you need or want. In the second and third options, you have to choose who will participate in decision making. In the fourth and fifth options, you meet with some or all of your employees as a group. This chapter concentrates on the last four options. It assumes that you will be seeking and using a number of participants in the decision-making process.

How to Choose Participants

There are two main reasons to invite an employee to participate:

1. The employee has information or knowledge relevant to the decision at hand.
2. The employee's acceptance of the decision is critical to implementation, and it's a good bet that he or she won't accept a unilateral decision.

Keep these reasons in mind when choosing participants. If you have a tendency to touch base with everyone in making a decision, resist it.

A secondary reason for inviting an employee to participate is developmental: You may want the employee to learn through participating. Even though he or she may be unable to contribute now, the training value of the process can be great. As long as you know what you expect the employee to learn—and he or she knows your expectations—by all means issue the invitation.

Forms of Involvement

According to Dr. George Huber of the University of Texas in his book *Managerial Decision Making*, involvement in the decision-making process can take one or more of these forms:

1. Exploring the problem
2. Generating alternatives
3. Making a choice

These forms reflect the three familiar stages of reaching a decision:

1. Identifying, defining, and diagnosing the problem
2. Generating alternative solutions to the problem
3. Evaluating and choosing among alternative solutions

Employees can be invited to participate in one, two, or all three of these stages by providing information, ideas, and suggestions. In the third stage, they can help to choose from among the solutions offered.

You should make it perfectly clear to employees what kind of involvement you want from them. For one thing, you are more likely to get the kind of input you need if they know what you expect. For another, you will reduce the likelihood of creating a false impression among them.

It's easy to create a false impression. You approach an employee and say something like, "Marilyn, I'd appreciate it if you'd give me a hand in solving this problem." What you really want is her help in suggesting alternatives (form/step 2). "Sure," says Marilyn happily. She walks away expecting to play a role in choosing a solution (form/step 3). When she finds out later what her actual role is to be, she feels deceived. The next time you ask her to participate, she is likely to be suspicious.

Such misunderstandings can be avoided. Explain precisely what role you expect an employee to play in the decision-making process. Never promise a greater role than is actually intended. You have to demonstrate that your participatory intentions are sincere. Moreover, they must *be* sincere. Don't misuse the participatory approach to try to manipulate employees to your way of thinking. They won't be fooled. They will view you as a shady operator. Smart managers are honest.

Six Pitfalls to Avoid

When participatory management involves dealing with a group, you face problems that don't occur in a one-on-one encounter. There are some very good reasons, according to N.R.F. Maier, why this is so. It's worth looking at some of the pitfalls you may encounter when conducting group meetings.

1. Social Pressure. Most employees want to be accepted by their peers. This desire promotes a tendency for them to want to agree with the opinion of the majority in a group. So strong is this tendency that many employees will agree with a majority opinion even when they regard it as a poor decision.

2. First-Solution Bias. The first sensible solution introduced into a group discussion frequently gets accepted by the group. For some reason, people are inclined to fasten on that first solution as the right one, even though better suggestions are offered later.

3. Individual Domination. One person may emerge in the group who captures more than his or her fair share of influence in the group's deliberations. The person may be verbally skilled, merely talk a lot, or just be mulishly stubborn. The dominant person in the group is sometimes the manager, which is regrettable because others in the group (remember how and why group members were chosen) may have better information, ideas, or suggestions to offer than the manager has.

4. Disagreement Leading to Hard Feelings. Conflict in a group can be good or bad. Some disagreement is to be expected. It's often an essential ingredient for obtaining innovative solutions. After all, if everyone agreed prior to the meeting, there might have been no need for the meeting in the first place. What can be harmful is disagreement that creates hard feelings among group members. As a manager, you should try to defuse any hard feelings, because residual bitterness can cause trouble when the time comes to implement the decision.

5. Conflicting Goals. Even though a group meeting is goal-oriented, don't assume that the sole aim of all members is to reach the goal. Conflicts can lie just below the surface. A dangerous kind of conflict is the one between personal goals and the goals of the business unit. For example, a group member may pull out all the stops in trying to win an argument regardless of the consequences to the group or business. The arguer is mainly trying to enhance his or her personal image as a power holder, a winner.

6. Failure to Protect Constructive Opinions. Group members bring with them different kinds of information, ideas, or suggestions. Some members' opinions are sound, some not so sound. Group members also bring with them different temperaments. Some people are accommodating, others are not. As the meeting proceeds, individual opinions begin to shift. When this occurs, you should make an effort to protect the opinions of particularly constructive (but perhaps overly accommodating) members of the group. The hazard is that the best ideas, the soundest opinions, the positions of those most likely to make a valuable contribution will get washed away in a tide of stridency or charisma or blather.

Three Guidelines for Managing Meetings

Weighty volumes have been written on how to conduct group meetings. The groaning shelfful of books testifies to the difficulty of the task. Yet a judicious manager, a manager with perception and common sense, should be able to conduct group meetings successfully with a bit of practice. Here are three general guidelines.

1. Take charge. You're the boss. You're the one in charge. You've called the meeting to accomplish an objective. Tell the group what that objective is. If possible, tell the group how to go about achieving the objective, including the criteria for evaluation. That "if possible" qualifier is necessary, because the situation may be so unstructured that you don't know. In such cases, the first step is to establish decision-making procedures and evaluation criteria. In sum, taking charge of the meeting means (a) formulating a plan and (b) communicating that plan to the group.

2. Exercise control. During the meeting, make sure the group adheres to your plan. Don't lose control. Restate your objectives and clarify them, if necessary. As the group moves in the intended direction, make your approval clear. If the group deviates from your plan in an unconstructive way, show your dissatisfaction. That doesn't mean calling names, intimidating the mavericks, or acting defensively. It means simply getting the group back on track.

3. Encourage quality participation. Encourage all members to contribute. Ask for opinions, evaluations, analyses, and, when appropriate, expressions of feelings. Direct the group, but don't dominate substantive discussions. You are the leader in this situation but not the all-knowing expert. Point out that group members are to think autonomously, not merely comply with your wishes (if they know your wishes). Show solidarity with the group. Try to make the members feel comfortable. Keep the atmosphere pleasant. If tensions mount, suggest a break, crack a joke or, if someone else does, go along with it.

Groupthink and Its Dangers

"Let us reason together" was one of President Lyndon Johnson's favorite lines. As a congressional leader, he had no peer at cajolery. As president in the wake of John F. Kennedy's death, he charted a course for disaster that won him early, near-unanimous approval among the cabinet, the Congress, and the people of the United States. He was viewed as the team leader par excellence, sort of the Bear Bryant of the Oval Office.

The dark side of teamwork is what Yale psychologist Irving Janis has called groupthink, or heedless conformity to the shared goals of the group. Presidents are especially prone to being victimized by groupthink, as many Washington observers have pointed out. Managers can easily fall victim to it, too, since employees are generally unwilling to disagree publicly with their manager's wishes. The manager, mistaking compliance for consensus, may do a number of foolish things. Keep LBJ in mind as you consider the dangers:

The manager may become overly optimistic and be willing to take extraordinary risks.

The manager may construct rationalizations so as to discount warnings and other negative feedback on decisions that have been made.

The manager may ignore the moral or ethical consequences of the solution.

Groupthink is not easy for the manager to detect. This is true partly because it commonly occurs in groups whose members get along well together and admire their manager. In such an atmosphere, it is easy for the manager to conclude that he or she can do no wrong.

One way to combat groupthink is to generate, if none exists, the kind of productive disagreement that forces me-tooers to become reluctant nay-sayers. For example, you sense that during a discussion the group is zeroing in too soon on a particular solution. No one is supporting an alternative solution that is arguably as good as, or better than, everybody's favorite. You halt the discussion and assign two group members to debate the merits of both possible solutions at the group's next meeting. By forcing someone to look at, study, and argue for the alternative solution, you have gone a long way toward overcoming groupthink in that single instance.

The Nominal Group Technique

Up to this point, the focus has been on free-flowing group discussions. But there are several techniques for channeling the flow of talk in predetermined ways. Some of these highly structured decision-making methods have been shown to produce excellent results, both in quality of output and in group acceptance of that output. One especially good method is the "Nominal Group Technique" developed by Dr. André Delbeq of the University of Santa Clara and Dr. Andrew Van de Ven of the University of Minnesota. It consists of five steps:

Step 1. Have the group members generate ideas in writing. Open the meeting by asking the members to take ten or twenty minutes to jot down their ideas on the issue at hand. They are not to talk to one another. This step has two clear benefits. It ensures that members will think uninterruptedly about the issue. It encourages each member's productivity because it (a) exhibits other group members vigorously attacking the task and (b) strongly suggests that the written ideas will later be presented and discussed.

Step 2. Have the group members share their ideas. Each group member presents his or her idea orally, reading or paraphrasing the notes. A group leader summarizes each person's contribution on a flip chart. The group leader doesn't editorialize, and no discussion is allowed. This step has three benefits. It puts each idea on an equal footing, since no deference is paid to the presenter's power or status. It depersonalizes the ideas, since they are listed anonymously on the flip chart. It tolerates conflicting, even bizarre ideas, since the lack of discussion prevents immediate rejection.

Step 3. Discuss the ideas in order. The group leader reads each idea aloud, one at a time. As the ideas are read, the group discusses each one. If anybody in the group doesn't understand an idea, the originator is asked to clarify it. In this way, each idea gets its fair share of time, and each idea is made clear to all group members. No one is subject to a hard sell, because the group leader accepts only clarifying information, not spot advertising, from the originator.

Step 4. Rank the ideas. Have each group member indicate by secret ballot what he or she feels are, say, the five best ideas on the flip chart—giving five points to the best idea, four to the next best, and so on down to one. The group leader then collects the ballots and records the votes. The highest total represents the *group's* choice as the best idea. Each group member has had an equal say in the outcome.

Step 5. Have the group discuss the vote. The main purpose of this step is to decide whether an additional round of voting is required to produce a clear-cut choice. The nominal group technique is easy to use for exploring problems, generating alternatives, or making choices. You should explain to your employees the use or uses to which the technique is being put. If employees aren't going to be involved in making a decision, they ought to know it.

Participating in the Three Rs

As you consider the possible uses of participatory management, you may overlook a very important one—the three basic Rs. There are good reasons for using the participatory approach in connection with the three Rs:

Some of the many decisions involved in applying the three Rs are far from routine.

The information for making the decisions cannot be standardized or centralized.

Decisions do not have to be made especially quickly.

Managers often lack sufficient information to make good decisions.

Employees can legimately make contributions to the decision-making process.

In some areas, there is a definite chance that employees will resist unilateral directives.

A specific example will show this process in action. In one business unit, the president wished to set performance requirements for a large group of technicians in similar kinds of jobs. He asked for the involvement of his employees, conducting a series of meetings with representatives of the technicians and their managers. He assigned group members the task of identifying common dimensions of the various jobs for which performance requirements could be set. The nominal group technique was then used to determine the projected final dimensions. Ten dimensions were chosen and presented to the president. He fully concurred with all ten, and asked that performance requirements for each job be set in a participatory manner for each dimension. The process worked smoothly. The president was pleased. So were the technicians and their managers, who felt (rightly) that what resulted was the direct product of their efforts.

Similar examples for the first two Rs are easy to come by, but for the third R—reward—they are rare indeed. Except when employees are unionized, management stoutly resists the notion of involving employees in designing their reward system. However, studies by Dr. Edward Lawler and his associates at the University of Southern California suggest that this resistance may be unwarranted. He has concluded that employees (outside the confines of a collective bargaining agreement) can invade management's sacred reward-system turf and make worthwhile participatory contributions. Move cautiously. Don't discount the possibility of participatory management applied to the third R—but don't jump in with both feet either. Not yet.

Stay within Bounds

The participatory approach has much to recommend it. Like any other tool, though, it can be misapplied. Just as you wouldn't use a wood chisel as a screwdriver, you should avoid using employee participants in unsuitable ways. For example, the president of a university would hardly appoint a professor of medieval history to participate in a task force charged with formulating strategy for investing the university's endowment. Old Dr. Gislebertus just wouldn't have the information or knowledge to make a useful contribution.

Tremendous benefits can be reaped from a participatory approach, but don't expect the impossible. A great many business decisions require narrowly focused expertise. To turn loose a group of bright amateurs in a situation demanding arcane technical knowledge will not result in effective decision making.

And thus two glittering chapters of promise end on a note of caution. Make sure your house is in order before you proceed with participatory management. It can indeed be a great boon—an eye-opening triumph—but without adequate care and preparation, it can also be a disastrous bust.

Ten Points to Remember

1. An employee invited to participate in decision-making should usually be one who possesses relevant information or knowledge, or one whose support will be critical to implementing the decision.

2. Participation in decision making can also be a valuable training tool.

3. Involvement in decision making can take one or more of these forms: (a) exploring the problem; (b) generating alternatives; (c) making a choice.

4. An employee should understand exactly what his or her role is in a participatory management situation.

5. Group meetings present many pitfalls, including pressure to conform, first-solution bias, individual domination, disagreements leading to hard feelings, and conflicting goals.

6. In a group meeting, a manager should (a) take charge, (b) exercise control, and (c) encourage quality participation.

7. Avoid being victimized by groupthink—compliance caused by the reluctance of employees to argue with their manager.

8. The nominal group technique is a simple, structured way to involve employees in decision making.

9. Many decisions involving the three Rs lend themselves to a participatory management approach.

10. For participatory management to work, a business unit must be in good shape, and the right people must be chosen.

13

How to Manage Your Own Career

I T was Calvin Coolidge who said, "The business of America is business." And so it is. The very picture of success in the United States, as television advertising makes clear, is the dynamic business leader. Given this, it's natural to assume that outstanding success as a manager equals personal happiness. And it often does. Research shows that job satisfaction usually increases as a person moves up the organizational ladder. But managerial success also comes with certain strings attached. The effort you expend on your job may take time away from other activities that are also sources of happiness. You may neglect your mental or physical well-being in the drive to succeed. You may slight valuable relationships with family and friends.

Managerial success may well bring with it power and prestige. It almost always brings money. The old adage about money not buying happiness is partly true, partly false. Everybody knows stories of desperately unhappy people with money. Howard Hughes in his final years was nobody's ideal of either success or happiness. Yet money in our society is clearly a vehicle for the pursuit of happiness. It may not buy happiness directly, but look at all the things it *will* buy! The catch is this: Most of those things require nonworking time if they are to be enjoyed. What good is a forty-foot yacht, except symbolically, if you have no time to take it out to sea. Personal happiness often demands a balance between the time spent gaining managerial success and the time spent enjoying it.

The reason for such a long windup before the pitch is that there are specific, definable ways to succeed as a manager. This chapter covers some of them. Along the way, you may begin to think, "Hey, that's a hard road!" Yes. It may be, in which case your basic concern may not be simply how to do it, but rather, "Do I *want* to do it?" That is anything but a trivial question. Regardless of your career stage, you should ask yourself what price you are willing to pay for managerial success.

This book assumes that you want to succeed as a manager. It does not claim that such success will inevitably lead to personal happiness. It can, but it may not. It's more likely to lead to personal happiness if you keep the rest of your life in balance. You can do that, to be sure, but you have to resolve to do it.

Focusing on You

Up to now, the emphasis in this book has been on how to manage employees effectively in a smooth-running business unit. The success of the business unit has been your goal. Now the focus shifts to you. The aim of the rest of the book is to show how to advance in your career. This is by no means a subtle shift of emphasis. The fact is that what is good for your career may *not* be good for your present business unit.

To take a familiar example: Cal Ehlers is a rising star in marketing at Apgar International. From sales representative to field manager, to regional manager, to assistant director of marketing, his ascent has been fast enough and steady enough to attract the interest of competing companies. One of them, Zanzibar, Inc., has just lost its director of marketing. The Zanzibar managers next in line are not quite ready for the job. Zanzibar, casting its net, hauls in Cal Ehlers for a series of interviews. They like him and offer him the job, which carries with it considerably more money, power, and prestige than he now has. He accepts.

The move is a good one for Cal Ehlers, but Apgar International loses. Their highflier has deserted them. This kind of thing happens all the time, of course. It is why business units are foolish to provide managers with so-called career development training programs that serve their employees' self-interest better than the business unit's interest.

Excel at Today's Job

Books on how to succeed in business are perennially popular. Some of them provide sound, practical advice, while the magic formulas touted by others are strictly for dreamers. One career management expert whose observations seem largely on target is Dr. Tim Hall of Boston University. His book, *Careers in Organizations*, presents a clear picture of what it takes to get ahead. Dr. Hall's ideas underlie many of the suggestions that follow.

The first suggestion may appear so obvious as to be frivolous. But it isn't the least bit frivolous. To some managers it isn't even obvious. To wit: *You must excel at your present job.* "Well, of course," you say. The sad fact is, however, that an occasional manager is so intent on advancing to the next step that he or she neglects the presumed basis for such advancement—the present job. That's a fairly big mistake unless the manager's dad owns the company, and maybe even then. Being a successful day-to-day manager is surely not all it takes to advance, but it is *one* of the things it takes. You must get the present job done right to prove that you can do the next one.

Develop Mobility

Good old Joe Sluffoff may get a gold watch for sitting at the same desk ad infinitum, but he won't get the brass ring. Assuming you are a successful manager, you didn't get there by being complacent. Don't be complacent now. Don't jog in place. Look ahead. Seek opportunities beyond the horizon. Here are five key rules for managers in search of the brass ring.

1. Maintain your options. Be a generalist. The people at the top of the pyramid, the senior managers, are generalists. They have to be. Don't allow yourself to become so specialized that you reduce your options for advancement. At certain stages of your career, you will need strong product and process knowledge. At each stage, view that knowledge as a stepping-stone, not as an end in itself. A technocrat in a staff position may be invaluable to the business unit, but he or she is poorly placed to advance to a slot in general management.

2. Don't be blocked by a going-nowhere boss. If your boss doesn't want to move up the ladder or has no prospects of doing so, make a move.

With the boss mired in mud, you'll go nowhere either. This can hurt in two ways, apart from preventing your direct-line advancement: (a) The boss is unlikely to help you develop your managerial skills by requiring higher or different types of performance from you. (b) The boss may need you to maintain his or her precarious position, in which case the last thing on the boss's self-protective mind is your career advancement.

3. Become crucial to an upwardly mobile boss. This is exactly where you want to be. If your boss wants to move up and has a chance of doing so, stay in there. Hang on to those coattails. Make sure he or she learns to rely on you. Excel at the fundamentals of your job. Perform special assignments that go well beyond basic requirements. Make sure that your efforts lead to significant, positive consequences for your boss.

4. Be visible. People are more likely to attend to your career if they know you exist. You cannot afford to be a lovely flower "born to blush unseen." Get noticed. Be heard. You may be the shy, reserved type, but don't just brood about the fact that the prickly thorns are getting all the attention. Go out there and join them. Volunteer for assignments and positions that give you visibility.

5. Quit a job on your own terms. Don't burn your bridges behind you when you move on to another position. Whether you move within your present business unit or outside it, never quit in a state of high emotion. (Or if you do, don't show it.) Never let your current position deteriorate to the point where you are forced out. When you move, you want to leave behind friends, not enemies. Above all, move at your own convenience.

Talk to Others about Your Career

The only thing harder than choosing a career in the first place is knowing how to manage one. You will probably find it much easier to oversee the careers of your employees than to oversee your own.

It sometimes pays to talk your situation over with family, friends, and co-workers. They see things from a different perspective, and that can often be helpful. If you have a mentor, he or she is a natural source. Professional vocational counselors may be of assistance, but choose wisely. Make sure the counselor has the necessary background and/or appropriate academic credentials (for instance, a Ph.D. in vocational psychology) and is experienced in working with managers.

Take Advantage of Luck

A few years ago, Kenny Rogers sang a mournful song about a dying gambler. Among the gambler's final bits of advice were to "know when to hold 'em" and "know when to fold 'em." That advice holds true in career management as well. Just as managerial success depends partly on luck, so does career success. Luck doesn't stand around waiting, though. It requires you to take note of it and, if possible, take advantage of it. Be prepared for the big chance. When opportunity knocks, open the door. The job opportunity that comes your way today may not exist tomorrow. Move!

Choose a Job Carefully

Remember the familiar advice of a Little League baseball coach: "You have to play the ball; don't let the ball play you." That advice, like the gambler's, applies to your career. You are, and must remain, the person in charge of any career change. Don't fall prey to an eager recruiter, a persuasive interviewer, or an affable prospective boss. Even when a job comes seeking you, it may be the wrong job. When you go looking outside your present business unit, you may get offers that demand a firm no. There are three main questions to ask yourself in regard to a major career move:

1. Do I have a good chance of being successful on the new job? In answering this, don't let optimism or self-confidence get in the way of common sense. Remember that it's much easier to succeed in a business unit that has a record of success than in one that doesn't. For example, let's say Gail Jones takes over as marketing manager in a firm with 40 percent of the microwidget market and steadily increasing sales over the past five years. At about the same time, Brenda Smith accepts a similar position in a firm with 20 percent of the same market and steadily declining sales over the past five years. Now, Brenda may be a whiz, but she will have an uphill struggle in her position, while Gail, whiz or not, will probably do well.

2. *Will the job help me to grow?* Will it sharpen your present abilities or add new ones? A new job should stretch you.

3. *Does the new job give me opportunities for advancement?* This is of critical importance, yet it may be very hard to determine. Give it a try anyway. If you are in a dead-end job now, you certainly don't want to move to another one. If the boss who's hiring you is immobile—something you may or may not be able to determine—remember prior warnings. A boss who's stuck in place is not the kind of boss you should be looking for.

Make Periodic Assessments

Having a definite career goal is essential to success. You have to pick a target to shoot at—but the target is almost sure to be a moving one. You can't possibly foresee all of the ups and downs that will occur during a thirty- or forty-year career. You will have to take time out now and then to reevaluate your aims and your progress. Try to figure out where you want to be, say, five or ten years down the road. Then determine what steps, including self-development activities, are most likely to get you there.

When making periodic assessments, keep in mind that not everyone gets to the top. This is not meant to be a counsel of despair. It merely recognizes the fact that when you first set your goal, you probably set it very high. Time and circumstances may alter it. You may conclude that you have reached the upper limits of your career growth, and that you should accept a less ambitious goal than you had originally set. This is a difficult assessment to make, but realism may demand it. Don't give up too easily, though. Everyone has temporary setbacks.

Whatever you decide during your periodic self-assessments, remember the key principle: *Know where you want to go.* If you know that, you can make plans, reach decisions. If you don't, if your future is just a hazy blur to you, there is no way to pursue it rationally. You must have a goal.

Manage Yourself

If you know where you want to go and have a general idea of the best route, there are some potent self-management strategies you can use. These strategies are explained in the literature of clinical psychology by such noted scholars as Dr. Albert Bandura of Stanford University and Dr. Frederick Kanfer of the University of Illinois. What Drs. Bandura and Kanfer describe are a number of practical applications of behavioral theory. Typically, the behavioral strategies have been used to treat a variety of clinical problems—smoking, overeating, disruptive classroom behavior. But they are equally useful in helping to control other kinds of behaviors and, because of that, can be a highly effective career-management device.

You don't have to buy the whole rats-in-a-maze package of behaviorism to make good use of the theory. In its practical form, think of it simply as self-management. In moving toward a career goal, you have to engage in certain behaviors. Self-management can help ensure that you do in fact engage in those behaviors. Recall the earlier suggestion that you should nominate yourself for special assignments. Doing so is a behavior. The specific kinds of assignments you seek out depend on your job and your career objectives, but the point is that self-nomination is a behavior, one that can move you toward those objectives. Behavior is action.

Self-management is a three-stage process:

- *Self-monitoring.* This means paying careful, deliberate attention to your own behavior. You can't just say that you *should* nominate yourself for a special assignment. You have to *do* it.
- *Self-evaluation.* You need to judge the effectiveness of what you do in light of the objective you are seeking. Did the special assignment go well? Was it noticed? Is the outcome likely to help further your career?
- *Self-reward.* If your self-evaluation shows that you have met or exceeded the objective, give yourself a reward. Let's say the special assignment has worked out well and produced the positive results you hoped for. You treat yourself to a Caribbean cruise or a camcorder.

If this procedure sounds pretty much like applying the three basic Rs to your own life, you're right.

Aim for an Immediate Goal

The word *goal* has been used up to this point to mean your long-range career target. But a goal can also be a specific, short-term behavior that you believe will move you toward that far-off result. In fact, a long-range goal, if it is to be manageable, must be broken down into a number of activities that can be accomplished in the short run. Self-management consists of setting and attaining these short-term goals. All of them are directed toward the ultimate goal and become a step-by-step path toward it.

Say you have a special assignment to write a report on your business unit's competitive advantages and disadvantages. The research is finished, and you are ready to start writing. Your *goal* is to write eight pages a day for each of the next four work days, thus completing what you expect to be a thirty-two-page report. Self-monitoring is easy enough—just count the pages you finish each day. Self-evaluation requires you to do no more than compare your cumulative count to your goal. Simpleminded? Not at all. Many people fail to meet goals because they don't measure their accomplishments and don't compare them to a predetermined standard.

Reward Your Own Efforts

With most self-management goals, you have no reason to expect your boss or anyone else to shout glad hosannas and shower you with ticker tape. Your reward comes in the form of self-satisfaction. You promised yourself eight pages a day, and you delivered on the promise. It makes you feel good.

Sometimes, though, you may want to give yourself a more tangible reward. Let's say you hate writing. Conversely, you love a particular imported beer. You make a contract with yourself: "If I finish eight pages of the report today, I'll treat myself to a bottle of Wunderbrau tonight." The tangible self-rewards people choose to regulate their own behavior vary widely: dinner with one's spouse at a favorite restaurant; an hour's worth of television viewing instead of an hour's worth of work at home in the evening; a new suit of clothes or a new dress. The reward itself is unimportant. What is important is that you get satisfaction from it *and* that you make payment only if you meet or exceed your goal. In other words, self-denial is part of self-management. You can probably afford a bottle of Wunderbrau whenever you want it. Not drinking it unless you've earned it is self-denial.

You may already use these self-management techniques. To some people—a very few—they come naturally. But most managers don't use them, and many are inclined to regard them as a bit silly. They're not. They're soundly grounded in behavioral psychology.

Self-management works. Give it a try.

Ten Points to Remember

1. Success as a manager is most likely to lead to personal happiness when a balance exists between work and leisure.

2. What is good for your managerial career may not be good for your present business unit.

3. You must excel at the job you have now if you expect to be considered for advancement.

4. To get ahead, be mobile: maintain options, sidestep a dead-end boss, become indispensable to a go-getting boss, be visible, and leave a job on your own terms.

5. Discuss your career aspirations with others who may be able to give helpful advice.

6. If opportunity knocks, don't hesitate to answer.

7. When you are offered a new job, determine its potential and its possible pitfalls as carefully as you can.

8. Make it a point to assess your career position from time to time, measuring your progress against your long-term goal.

9. Use self-management techniques—including self-monitoring, self-evaluation, and self-reward—to advance your career.

10. Set and attain a series of immediate, short-term goals, with appropriate self-rewards, as part of your long-term career-management strategy.

14

Keys to Self-development

O NE way to discover the elements that lead to the top in any field is to study the lives of those who have gotten there. Many researchers have done this. They have pored over the biographies of towering figures from Alexander the Great to Douglas MacArthur, from John D. Rockefeller to Lee Iacocca. What have they found? Not surprisingly, they have found that certain traits and tactics are common to most men and women who direct the actions of others.

For one thing, leaders are self-confident. No surprise there—a leader cannot hang back. For another, leaders are skilled at making favorable impressions. Not only do they view themselves as winners, but so do their associates. And finally, they know how to use power advantageously. Of the myriad skills in the successful manager's repertoire, the effective use of power is perhaps the trickiest. Power can be exercised blatantly or subtly, foolishly or well. So fascinating and complex is the subject that entire books have been written on it. This chapter hits only the high spots.

Conquer Your Doubts

Anyone who has seen the stage play or movie *How to Succeed in Business Without Really Trying* will remember the scene in which Finch, played by Robert Morse, gazes admiringly into a washroom mirror and sings, "I Believe in You." You should also believe in you. It's crucial. You can have all the career-relevant skills, abilities, knowledge, and information in the world, but you won't get far without self-confidence.

Unfortunately, self-confidence doesn't come in a cellophane-wrapped package to pluck off a shelf. To say "You have to have self-confidence" may sound a little like the English teacher telling a terrified valedictorian, about to speak to a thousand parents at graduation, "Now, don't be nervous, Janet." Don't be nervous? Is that guy kidding? Of course Janet is nervous.

Still, there are ways to overcome stage fright, just as there are ways to overcome a more general lack of self-confidence. The techniques are similar. Both are based on increased knowledge and experience.

Ted Braverman is a supervisor at Futurex Plastics Company. To take the next step up, Ted realizes he will have to be able to do financial analyses. Math is not Ted's strong suit, and he fears the prospect of the math that financial analyses entail. But he refuses to be stopped. Knowing that he must develop his ability in math, he signs up for an evening course at a nearby college: Introduction to Business Mathematics. Ted struggles with the course—he knew it would be hard for him—but he comes through with a B. Not only has he learned the math he needs in order to advance, he has also boosted his self-confidence. He is ready for the next stepping-stone.

The Classroom, the Library

Since knowledge and experience contribute to self-confidence, you are likely to find that your two best choices for self-development, apart from a job change or in-house training, are (a) the classroom and (b) the library. The courses and reading materials you choose should be chosen to help you fulfill your assessed needs. A course on accounting for nonaccountants, for instance, is generally more useful, if less fun, than one on fly-fishing and bait-casting. Courses at a local college or university may earn you credits toward a degree, or they may be noncredit short courses. Which courses are best for you will depend on your needs analysis.

It would be an obvious plus if specific guidance could be given on how to do a needs analysis. Sad to say, very little is known about assessing personal developmental needs. It's good advice (but a truism) to suggest that you be honest and open with yourself when comparing your present skills with those demanded by the target you are aiming for. It's sensible (but repetitive) to say that it often pays to talk over your career plans with others. The best approach to evaluating a course or a book (where again there is no research to draw on) may be simply gut reaction. Do you feel more self-confident after having read a certain book or taken a particular course? If so, it was probably worthwhile. That approach won't pass muster as science, but it has some commonsense validity.

Self-development is a lifelong process. As your job changes, your needs change. As your career target moves, you will need to reposition yourself through self-development. Note that the word is *self*-development. Don't count on your business unit to supply all, or in some cases any, of the training you need. It's your career; it's your responsibility.

Making an Impression

You must also take the lead in making yourself visible. This was mentioned earlier. Now it needs to be stressed more strongly, because without visibility, your career advancement will die aborning. Indeed, it is fair to say that *the impressions others have of you are likely to be more important to your career than your actual accomplishments*.

People will make decisions about your career that are based on their impressions of you—and those impressions may not square with the facts. Quite candidly, looking and talking like a CEO probably have as much to do with your gaining the position as do your qualifications.

This raises a couple of disturbing questions. The first one is, doesn't it fly in the face of everything that has been said in this book about the four Rs and the system of formal, objective appraisal that presumably is in place? Not really. An example will show why.

There are five senior operating managers at Oceanus Marine Equipment, Inc. They have all worked their way up the organizational ladder. Their track records, all excellent, have been examined closely on the occasion of each promotion and on a more regular basis as well. The five managers have been through such scrutiny four or five times, and each time they have surpassed their less qualified peers. On paper, each one has the qualifications for filling the soon-to-be-vacant CEO position. As you can see, the appraisal system is in place, and it has worked. But what now? Who gets the top job? The smart money would certainly have to bet on the senior operating manager who has created the best impression.

The second question is an ethical one. Is it desirable that more-or-less superficial impressions, or images, carry the weight they do in modern business, even in the example above, and is a backlash against this "imaging" likely to occur? A few years ago, Christopher Lasch wrote in *The Culture of Narcissism* that "the upwardly mobile corporate executive . . . advances through the corporate ranks not by serving the organization but by convincing his associates that he has the attributes of a 'winner.'" How true is that in your own experience? Is it an overstatement? Certainly, too great an emphasis on the slick and the facile serves neither business nor society very well. Yet you, as a manager, have to work within the parameters that exist. You cannot build yourself a separate ivory tower.

To have a reasonable chance of promotion, you will have to be visible to the "significant others" within your business unit. They must have a distinct impression of you—a *good* impression. A negative impression can consign you to oblivion just as surely as no impression at all. How does a manager get saddled with a negative impression? In a number of ways:

Some managers, highly visible, are at the same time poor performers. A manager who is a poor performer—and is seen as one—is in trouble.

Even successful managers can create a poor impression. Dr. David Kipnis of Temple University and his associates have repeatedly demonstrated through their research that a boss will form a negative impression of a subordinate who seems to be performing well for some reason other than his or her ability or personal effort. In other words, if you succeed (or the boss thinks you do) because of lucky breaks or anything else beyond your direct control, your image will suffer.

Inconsistency of performance can lead to negative impressions. A manager whose performance varies from very high to very low, but on the average is good, will be viewed as less effective than the manager whose performance is also good but is more consistent, lacking peaks and valleys.

And this research finding, perhaps from the College of Recent Presidents: Managers who alter their course when proven wrong are seen in a less favorable light than those who stick to their guns in the face of adversity.

Finally, how a manager looks and talks makes a difference. A manager who wears a shiny suit and talks in a squeaky voice will create a negative impression apart from any other aspects of his performance.

The image you want to project is that of (a) a consistently good performer, (b) one whose success stems from ability and inward drive, and (c) a decisive person willing to stick to a course of action when the going gets rough. How do you present that kind of image? Definitely not by being modest. Not by saying, "It was really pretty easy," or "I had a lot of luck."

You have to be your own PR person. You should tactfully broadcast your successes and, in doing so, place yourself in the most favorable light possible. *Never* downgrade the role you have played. *Always* emphasize your strengths, but do so without seeming to boast.

Also, don't neglect your physical appearance. A successful manager should look the part. Had you chosen to be a sheepherder, your appearance would hardly matter. But having chosen to be a manager, you must look and dress the part. Like it or not, your appearance will be judged, consciously or unconsciously, against other managers in your business unit.

On the Uses of Power

Power is your potential for influencing the actions of other people. By its very nature, management involves the use of power. A standard definition of management—getting work done through others—illustrates the point. Power can be exercised upward (and laterally) as well as downward. You may find that your skill in influencing your boss has as much to do with your eventual success as your authority over subordinates.

As you move up the organizational ladder, you will gain more and more "legitimate" power—the power that goes with the position you occupy. Don't overestimate this power. It will help you very little in exerting influence upward, and it may prove less effective than you expect in regulating the behavior of your employees.

The classic works of Dr. John French of the University of Michigan and Dr. Bertram Raven of UCLA identify the main sources of managerial power. Since your use of power will have a significant impact on your career, you will want to give some thought to the three sources of power you have over employees.

1.   *Reward power* comes from your ability to allot pay, praise, and other incentives among your employees. This power was covered at length in chapter 6. The important principle is that your power to mediate rewards enhances your power to get employees to do what you want them to do.

2.   *Referent power* comes from your employees' personal identification with you. If you have referent power, your employees value your friendship, look up to you, and comply with your requests out of personal admiration. That sounds like heaven, doesn't it? The catch is that, like heaven, it can't be reached at a single bound, and some managers can't get there at all. To acquire referent power, you have to encourage friendship, yet at the same time retain your status as a manager in the eyes of your employees. It can be a high-wire act. If you keep your balance well enough, there are obvious benefits: your employees carry out your wishes, and a certain warmth and rapport exist between you and them.

3.   *Coercive power* is drill-sergeant power. It stems from your ability to discipline, even punish your subordinates. Its use will ordinarily produce employee compliance, at least to a degree, but it reduces your attractiveness as a manager, destroying your chances to establish referent power and hampering your ability to maximize reward power. Who wants to get praise from a plug-ugly boss? Even the employees' apparent compliance with your wishes is little more than a public pose. Unless you maintain close surveillance, coerced employees are not likely to be eager and productive workers.

A fourth type of power, *expert power,* may be used to influence either employees or supervisors. Expert power is based on your unique knowledge, information, and expertise. Just being an expert, though, is not enough. An employee or supervisor must also believe in your honesty, your truthfulness, and your willingness to communicate, for the expertise of a devious game-player can be used in deadly ways. Expert power, like referent power, is an ideal base to use in exerting influence upward.

The Management of Stress

As a manager, you cannot avoid stress. Inevitably, you will take risks and feel apprehensive about them. That is one of the costs of being career-minded. A few years ago, the senior author and two colleagues wrote a book, *Managing Job Stress*, that identifies the causes and consequences of job-related stress. Both lists are remarkably long. Working can be hazardous to your health, especially your mental health.

Let's skip the causes (which you know exist) and go straight to some of the cures, or, more accurately, the ways of coping. This list is far from exhaustive, but it does indicate that there are many practical ways to deal with stress.

1. Social Support. When the going gets rough, turn to a friend. You will find it very helpful to talk with someone who is approachable, trustworthy, cooperative, and warm. Your friend may be a family member, a neighbor, a co-worker, or even your boss. Don't keep stress to yourself; talk about your problems. It works.

2. Relaxation Techniques. When faced with stress, you can turn to any one of a number of useful techniques:

Progressive relaxation

Relaxation response

Meditation

Biofeedback

Any of these, *if taken seriously*, can work for you. According to Dr. Herbert Benson and his associates at Harvard Medical School, the various relaxation methods have these features in common:

A quiet environment

A mental device, such as silently repeating a sound or fixing your gaze, that causes you to shift your thinking away from its usual, rational, external focus

A passive attitude that allows you to ignore distractions (including the distraction of trying to perform well at relaxing!)

A comfortable position

Don't get hung up on the mechanics of relaxing. You don't need a seminar or a psychologist or a Tibetan holy man to teach you how to relax. Nor do you need a basement full of equipment. All you must have is the desire to do it and a willingness to take the time. If you think you're too *busy* to relax, that's prima facie evidence of your *need* to relax.

3. Exercise. Some evidence suggests that a regular program of exercise can help you cope with stress. However, if you really don't like exercise, you probably won't gain much relaxation from doing it. There's no point in turning play into work.

4. Psychodynamic Counseling. This form of therapy is aimed at helping you gain insight into your difficulties and using this new understanding to make changes for the better. Popular approaches include Freud's psychoanalysis, Rogers' client-centered therapy, Frankl's logotherapy, and Ellis' rational–emotional therapy. How do you choose the best psychodynamic approach for your own situation? Good question, one with no easy answer. How do you choose a counselor who is qualified in the approach you need? Another good question. Before going into psychodynamic counseling, you will have to do quite a bit of preliminary investigation.

5. Behavior Counseling. Unlike psychodynamic approaches, behavior counseling does not focus on gaining insight into your problems. Instead, it concentrates on changing your future behavior patterns. Common methods include desensitization, aversion training, assertiveness training, and self-management. Behavior counseling has proved to work well in helping people cope with various kinds of behavioral problems. As with any kind of counseling, however, the choice of the right counselor is critical.

6. Withdrawal. If career-related stress problems become unmanageable, you may have to withdraw from the situation, either psychologically or physically. It's painful to lower your career aspirations or to change jobs, but in the long run it may be less painful than toughing it out through aggression, alcohol, or some other self-defeating response. If you have truly reached an impasse, admit it and find another route.

On the other hand, you don't want to give up every time the road gets a little rocky. Withdrawing repeatedly in the face of stress is in itself harmful.

Do what you have to do about stress, keeping always in mind that your career is only one part of your life. If your career so dominates your thoughts that it becomes a constant source of pressure, then success on the job is probably not going to make you happy anyway. In that case, it behooves you to explore your options.

Onward and Upward

From power to stress to . . . what? This book has covered a lot of ground in a limited amount of space. It has touched briefly on a great many management techniques that research has shown to work. It has mentioned a number of outstanding researchers along the way, but it has seldom gone into much detail about their writings. Nor has it mentioned many of the other outstanding books on business management. The Appendix remedies that situation, discussing briefly a number of books whose content parallels to some extent, and usually amplifies, the content of this book. More than that, it provides a reading list that goes far beyond the *One Incredible Power Technique That Wins You Super-manager Status Instantly* kind of book that promises more in its title than it can possibly deliver. Although annotated reading lists score well down on the scale of most people's favorite literature (that's a guess, not a research finding), you will find it worthwhile to skim through the one that follows. It's a gold mine.

Ten Points to Remember

1. To advance as a manager, you must be self-confident; you must believe in your ability to lead.
2. You can increase your self-confidence by increasing your knowledge and experience.
3. In choosing a course to take or a book to read, pay close attention to the specific need you want to address.
4. The impression you make on others is one of the most important aspects of career management; a good image is essential.

5. Become your own PR person, tactfully emphasizing your strengths, attributing nothing to luck, and paying close attention to your personal appearance.

6. Management, which involves getting work done through others, requires the acquisition and effective use of power.

7. Of the three kinds of power over employees, reward power and referent power are much more productive and desirable than coercive power.

8. Expert power, based on expertise, is also valuable at all levels within the business.

9. Since it is impossible to avoid stress as a manager, you should be aware of the various ways of controlling it.

10. Keep in mind that your career, important as it is, comprises only one part of your life; success at all costs is hollow.

Appendix:
The Smart Manager's
Library

Managing Smart is a concise guide. Every topic in the book has been covered at greater length elsewhere. There are probably some topics you would like to explore in more depth, and this chapter shows you where to look. The books listed here can be considered the core of the smart manager's library.

The books are arranged in the order in which the topics appear in *Managing Smart*, and chapter references are noted. For example, books about performance training appear under the head of "Training Methods That Work." The chapter references are 9 and 10.

Thousands of books have been written about business management. More appear every day. As a consequence, this list is extremely limited, containing only books that are (a) among the best of their kind and (b) readable by people who are not specialists in the area of human resources management. While many excellent books may have been slighted, no bad books have been included. Every book on the list is recommended.

Basics of Management
(Chapter 1)

These books provide a starting point for understanding the history and current status of management practices in the United States.

- *Managing Organizational Behavior*, by Ramon J. Aldag and Arthur P. Brief. St. Paul: West Publishing Co., 1981. This is a standard college textbook on organizational behavior. If the topic is new to you, this book will provide a good introduction. Chapter 2 is especially useful, presenting a brief overview of the discipline and its relevance to the practice of management.

- *The Principles of Scientific Management*, by Frederick W. Taylor. New York: Harper and Brothers, 1911.
- *The Functions of the Executive*, by Chester I. Barnard. Cambridge, Mass.: Harvard University Press, 1938.
- *My Years with General Motors*, by Alfred P. Sloan. Garden City, N.Y.: Doubleday, 1964.

These books, taken together, offer a superb history of American management. More important, the ideas expressed capture the essence of what *Managing Smart* calls the basics. Taylor, an industrial engineer, is regarded as the father of scientific management. Barnard, for many years president of New Jersey Bell, developed a comprehensive theory of management, while Sloan, long-time president of General Motors, was a master of corporate organization and structure.

Requiring People to Perform
(Chapters 2 and 3)

These books deal with the question of what performance is all about. They stress the need for performance requirements and tell how to set those requirements.

- *The Practice of Management*, by Peter F. Drucker. New York: Harper and Row, 1954. Drucker, Professor Emeritus at New York University, emphasizes the necessity of establishing performance requirements and shows how this practice can become an integral part of managing a business unit.
- *Goal Setting: A Motivational Technique That Works!*, by Edwin A. Locke and Gary P. Latham. Englewood Cliffs, N.J.: Prentice–Hall, 1984. The exclamation point in the title is justified. This is the best book available on how to set performance requirements.

Job Performance and How to Review It
(Chapters 4 and 5)

Performance appraisal is one of the cornerstones of effective management. These books explain it in detail.

- *Performance in Organizations: Determinants and Appraisal*, by L.L. Cummings and Donald P. Schwab. Glenview, Ill.: Scott, Foresman, 1973. This book presents a fine conceptual model for understanding the elements of job performance. It also raises a number of important issues to consider in the design of appraisal systems.

- *Performance Appraisal and Review Systems: The Identification, Measurement and Development of Performance in Organizations*, by Stephen J. Carroll and Craig E. Schneier. Glenview, Ill.: Scott, Foresman, 1982. The ponderous title notwithstanding, you won't find a better, more readable book on how to design, implement, and evaluate appraisal systems. For the manager who wants to initiate a performance appraisal system, this book is must reading.

The Ways to Pay
(Chapters 6 and 7)

Employee compensation is the key to rewarding top performance and improving marginal performance. These two books deal with the topic.

- *Pay and Organizational Development*, by Edward E. Lawler III. Reading, Mass.: Addison–Wesley, 1981. Lawler may well be *the* expert on pay. His book specifies many of the compensation options available and notes their likely consequences.

- *Pay: Employee Compensation and Incentive Plans*, by T.H. Patten. New York: Free Press, 1977. Patten's is one of several good explanations of the mechanics of pay systems. Considerably more detailed than Lawler's, this book effectively complements his.

Wanted: Outstanding Employees
(Chapter 8)

How do you choose employees who can earn your respect? The task has never been easy, but the following books offer a great many perceptive answers.

- *Staffing Organizations*, by Benjamin Schneider. Pacific Palisades, Calif.: Goodyear Publishing, 1976. Schneider provides the most articulate and comprehensive overview of employee selection available. This is a must-read book.

- *Organizational Entry: Recruitment, Selection, and the Socialization of Newcomers*, by John P. Wanous. Reading, Mass.: Addison–Wesley, 1980. If you want to know more about creating realistic expectations on the part of new employees, this is the book to read. It's the only one on the topic.

- *Fairness in Selecting Employees*, by Richard D. Arvey. Reading, Mass.: Addison–Wesley, 1979. Hiring practices raise legal issues. Arvey presents a scary picture to managers who still rely exclusively on the job interview as a selection tool.

- *Costing Human Resources: The Financial Impact of Behavior in Organizations*, by Wayne F. Cascio. Boston: Kent Publishing, 1982. This is not light reading, but Cascio has the topic all to himself. No other book covers it. If you want to get an idea of the dollar impact of various human resources practices, this is your book.

Training Methods That Work
(Chapters 9 and 10)

The task of developing employees you can respect is a vital aspect of smart management. These books can help.

- *Training: Program Development and Evaluation*, by Irving L. Goldstein. Monterey, Calif.: Brooks/Cole, 1974. Although this is a very short book, it is probably the best one in print on the topic. In an evening or two of reading, you will gain a remarkable amount of information about training.

- *Developing and Training Human Resources in Organizations*, by Kenneth H. Wexley and Gary P. Latham. Glenview, Ill.: Scott, Foresman, 1981. This is essentially an updated and expanded version of what Goldstein says. The material on management development (chapters 8 and 9) is questionable, but overall the book is a worthwhile supplement to Goldstein.

Aspects of Leadership
(Chapters 11 and 12)

It may seem paradoxical, but participatory management demands exceptional leadership. Despite hundreds of books on the topic of leadership, only a few are first-rate.

- *Managerial Process and Organizational Behavior*, by Alan C. Filley and Robert J. House. Glenview, Ill.: Scott, Foresman, 1969. This is a standard college text, but the authors' chapters on leadership are perhaps the best ever written.
- *Leadership and Decision Making*, by Victor H. Vroom and Philip W. Yetton. Pittsburgh: University of Pittsburgh Press, 1973. A very hard book to read, it nevertheless qualifies as a must for managers who want to formulate a participatory strategy. You can skip over some of the technical details, but pay close attention when the authors get into the how-to part.
- *Managerial Decision Making*, by George P. Huber. Glenview, Ill.: Scott, Foresman, 1980. Books on decision making resemble the classic definition of television—a vast wasteland. Most decision-making books that are readable are also almost totally devoid of content. Huber's is an exception. Far from perfect, it is nonetheless readable, pragmatic, and useful.
- *Group Techniques for Program Planning*, by André L. Delbeq, Andrew H. Van de Ven, and David H. Gustafson. Glenview, Ill.: Scott, Foresman, 1975. If you want to use the nominal group technique, you must read this book. It's a jewel.

Self-management for Success
(Chapters 13 and 14)

There will never be a shortage of books on self-management, but many of them are fluff. The three books listed here have solid substance.

- *Careers in Organizations*, by Douglas T. Hall. Santa Monica, Calif.: Goodyear Publishing, 1976. This is the most comprehensive and honest book on careers that has been written in a long time. It is important reading.
- *Career Success/Personal Failure*, by Abraham K. Korman with Rhoda W. Korman. Englewood Cliffs, N.J.: Prentice–Hall, 1980. Korman and Korman have written a powerful book on the costs of being too career-minded. If you have that tendency, read it now.
- *Managing Job Stress*, by Arthur P. Brief, Randall S. Schuler, and Mary Van Sell. Boston: Little, Brown, 1981. Most books on job stress concentrate on the latest fad. This book doesn't. It is a serious look at a serious topic, with an excellent bibliography.

The foregoing books are the core of the smart manager's library. But they are only the core. The continuing need for development as a manager cannot be stressed too strongly. While the books listed here contain a wealth of useful information, your base of knowledge will grow as you advance in your career. Valuable new books will appear. As they do—and as you progress—you will want to read other books, adding the best of them to this core list.

Index

About the Authors

ARTHUR P. BRIEF is professor of management and organizational behavior at New York University's Graduate School of Business Administration. He has lectured throughout the United States, and he taught organizational behavior in the People's Republic of China in 1981 and 1982.

Professor Brief has authored more than seventy-five articles and chapters based on his studies of employee attitudes and behaviors. His previous five books address such diverse human resource management topics as task design, job stress, and productivity research. He is co-editor of Lexington Books' Issues in Organization and Management Series, which comprises books on theory, research, and practice, and editor of a series of books on administrative science for Garland Publishing Company. He has served on the editorial boards of several journals, including the *Academy of Management Review* and the *Academy of Management Journal*. Professor Brief is a Fellow of the American Psychological Association, past president of the Midwest Academy of Management, founding co-chairperson of the Academy of Management's Public Sector Division, and a member of the American Sociological Association and American Society for Personnel Administration.

Professor Brief is also an active advisor to management in the human resources area. In his role as a consultant, he has served a variety of industries, including health care, commercial banking, legal services, insurance, manufacturing, retailing, and publishing. He received his Ph.D. from the University of Wisconsin–Madison.

GERALD TOMLINSON is a writer and editor. Specializing in business and education, he has held various editorial and managerial positions in book publishing, including that of executive editor. His nonfiction includes two books on writing effective business letters, published by Prentice–Hall. The author of a recent mystery novel, *On a Field of Black*, he has written dozens of mystery stories that have appeared in *Ellery Queen's*, *Alfred Hitchcock's*, and other mystery magazines. Mr. Tomlinson graduated from Marietta College and attended Columbia Law School.